PENGUIN BOOKS

Test Your Prepositions

Alejandro Gómez Pasco
Lindavista DF
11·Aug· 2000

Test Your Prepositions

**Peter Watcyn-Jones
and Jake Allsop**

Illustrated by Ross Thomson

PENGUIN ENGLISH

PENGUIN ENGLISH

Published by the Penguin Group
Penguin Books Ltd, 27 Wrights Lane, London W8 5TZ, England
Penguin Books USA Inc., 375 Hudson Street, New York, New York 10014, USA
Penguin Books Australia Ltd, Ringwood, Victoria, Australia
Penguin Books Canada Ltd, 10 Alcorn Avenue, Toronto, Ontario, Canada M4V 3B2
Penguin Books (NZ) Ltd, 182-190 Wairau Road, Auckland 10, New Zealand

Penguin Books Ltd, Registered Offices: Harmondsworth, Middlesex, England

First published 1990
10 9 8 7 6 5 4 3

Test 49 is from *The Book of Nasty Legends* by Paul Smith and is reproduced by permission
of Routledge

Filmset in Century Schoolbook

Made and printed in Great Britain by
BPCC Hazell Books
Aylesbury, Bucks, England
Member of BPCC Ltd

INTRODUCTION

For the majority of students, learning English prepositions is both very difficult and very time-consuming. *Test Your Prepositions* tries to tackle this problem by providing concentrated practice on various prepositions in a stimulating and interesting way. Altogether 970 items are tested, ranging from prepositions followed by nouns to prepositions after adjectives, verbs and nouns, to prepositions of place and time to phrasal verbs and idioms.

Test Your Prepositions forms part of the Test Your Vocabulary series and, in keeping with the series, the emphasis is on variety, with tests ranging from gap-filling exercises to multiple-choice, crosswords, rewriting sentences, cartoons, word association, finding the misprints in newspaper headlines, and so on. There is even a test where the student has to fill in the missing prepositions in various jokes. (Who said learning prepositions has to be boring!)

Test Your Prepositions is for intermediate/advanced learners and can be used in class with a teacher or for self-study. To facilitate the latter, answers to the tests are included at the back of the book.

TO THE STUDENT

This book will help you to learn or consolidate a large number of prepositions. But in order for the new prepositions to become "fixed" in your mind, you will need to test yourself again and again. Here is one method you can use to help you learn these new prepositions.

1 Read the instructions carefully and try the test, writing your answers **in pencil**.
2 When you have finished, check your answers and correct any mistakes you have made. Pay special attention to the prepositions you didn't know or got wrong.
3 Try the test again 5–10 minutes later. You can cover up your answers or get a friend to test you. Repeat this until you can remember all the prepositions.
4 **Rub out your answers.**
5 Try the test again the following day. Again pay special attention to any prepositions that cause difficulty. (You might even try making up your own sentences with the "difficult" prepositions.)
6 Finally, plan to try the test at least twice within the following month. After this, most of the prepositions should be "fixed" in your mind.

CONTENTS

Prepositions of place   1

Look at the drawing and fill in the missing prepositions in the sentences below. Choose from the following (use each once only):

above	between	inside	to the left of
behind	in	on	to the right of
below	in front of	opposite	under

1   The sofa is .... the armchair.

2   The clock is .... the mantelpiece.

3   The magazine .... the table.

4   The painting is .... the fireplace.

5   The bookcase is .... the fireplace.

6   The book is .... the vase of flowers.

7   There are lots of books .... the bookcase.

8   The coffee table is .... the sofa and the armchair.

9   The cat is .... the armchair.

10 The goldfish is .... the goldfish bowl.

11 The record-player is .... the records.

12 The clock is .... the painting.

2 Choose the preposition 1: at, by, for, in

*Complete the following sentences using **at**, **by**, **for** or **in**.*

1 He sent a copy of his will to his bank .... safe keeping.

2 The house is to be sold .... auction.

3 Although I practise quite a lot, I never seem to win very often .... tennis.

4 Let Albert work it out; he has an aptitude .... figures.

5 You could tell .... a glance that he was no ordinary speaker.

6 Most people think the government is to blame .... rising unemployment.

7 Although their marriage was not a happy one, they decided to stay together .... the sake of the children.

8 There has been a sharp increase .... house prices in recent months.

9 They began to drop out of the race one .... one.

10 Do you know of a cure .... baldness?

11 She takes great pride .... her work.

12 He was the sort of person who immediately made you feel .... ease.

13 Did she give you any reason .... her behaviour?

14 I'm sorry, but I'm not .... liberty to tell you any more.

15 John's got very strange taste .... clothes, hasn't he?

16 Could you come back in half an hour? Mr Baston's .... lunch at the moment.

17 We didn't know .... certain whether they would come or not.

18 Think of a number. Now multiply it .... seven.

19 Do sit down. Mr Brown will join you .... a moment.

20 The attendance .... Saturday's meeting was very poor.

3 Prepositions of time

Read through the following and fill in the numbered blanks with a suitable preposition of time. Be careful, however, because in one or two cases no preposition is needed!

My parents met (1) .... the war: (2) .... August 1943 to be precise. My father was home (3) .... leave (4) .... the front, and he decided to spend the first week with his aunt in Liverpool. He hadn't seen her (5) .... several years, even though she had brought him up (6) .... his mother's death. Liverpool is not the most beautiful city in the world, but it can be very pleasant (7) .... summertime, especially early (8) .... the morning. (9) .... this particular morning, however, my father was in no mood to enjoy the sunrise over the Mersey. His train left Euston Station (10) .... time, at midnight, but (11) .... the time it got to Crewe, it was already three and a half hours (12) .... schedule. So he was in a bad mood and very tired (13) .... arrival at Lime Street Station. But something happened (14) .... minutes of his arrival that changed not only his mood but also his whole life. Feeling thirsty (15) .... his long journey, he decided to go and have a cup of tea in the station buffet. Typically, it was shut (16) .... that early hour. A notice on the door read "Opening hours: (17) .... 7 a.m. (18) .... 5.30 p.m. He looked at the station clock: ten (19) .... seven. The buffet should be open (20) .... now, he thought. But, knowing station buffets, he realised that he could wait (21) .... 8 or even 9 o'clock before it opened. Suddenly he noticed a pretty girl sitting on a bench. She was pouring some hot liquid from a thermos flask into a cup. Being something of a lady's man, my father (at least this is what my mother told me (22) .... some years later) sat down and said, "I've never seen such a pretty girl (23) :.................. all my life as you. And I haven't had a hot drink (24) .... last night. If you give me a drink of your tea, I'll marry you and look after you (25) .... the rest of your life!" Believe it or not, she smiled at him, gave him the tea, and ... well, I wouldn't be here (26) .... now if the buffet hadn't been shut (27) .... that fateful day (28) .... August 1943.

4 Complete the sentences

Complete the following sentences. Choose a suitable ending from those marked a–p.

1 My brother is very conscious ...

2 He was arrested ...

3 In Britain, having more than two wives at the same time is ...

4 The police charged the man ...

5 Most children are fond ...

6 The three men were found guilty ...

7 Since the weather was so bad, we decided ...

8 He apologised ...

9 Since Mrs Smith is ill, Mr Bond is deputising ...

10 He didn't want her to go, so he tried to prevent her ...

11 Since he had missed so many lessons, he was discouraged ...

12 She takes great pride ...

13 He tried to coax her ...

14 He complimented her ...

15 He was always very nervous ...

16 To tell you the truth, I'm not very keen ...

a from taking the exam.

b on her work.

c for his bad behaviour.

d for robbing a bank.

e against going to the beach.

f for her today.

g into going to the party.

h of his big nose.

i of going to the circus.

j from leaving.

k about going to the dentist.

l with murder.

m of fraud.

n in her work.

o on going out tonight.

p against the law.

Write your answers here:

1	2	3	4	5	6	7	8	9	10	11	12	13	14	15	16

Read through the sentences below and complete the crossword. The missing words are either adjectives or prepositions.

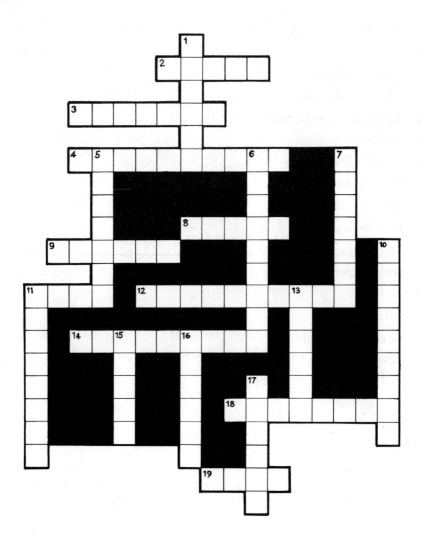

ACROSS

2 We're having a party on Saturday and I'm really excited .... it (5).

3 We thought he was a confirmed bachelor, so we were really surprised when we heard that he had got .... to a Swedish au pair girl (7).

4 He found it quite difficult to drive in France at first, because he was not .... to driving on the right (10).

8 Everyone felt .... for him because he was blind (5).

9 Peter has always been .... of the dark, and that's why he sleeps with the lights on (6).

11 I'm not very .... at tennis; I always seem to lose (4).

12 The businessman had been .... in all his business deals. He hadn't once failed to get an order (10).

14 If you're not .... with the service at the hotel, then you should complain to the manager (9).

18 My sister doesn't think that guns are very .... toys for children. If she had her way, they'd all be banned (8).

19 The boss has been ill .... a cold for the past week (4).

DOWN

1 You are not allowed to be .... from school without permission (6).

5 When the children woke up on Christmas morning, they were thrilled to see the ground .... with snow (7).

6 She was so .... in her newspaper that she didn't notice me come in (9).

7 James is late again. That's .... of him. I don't think he's ever been early for anything in his entire life! (7)

10 Looking at the way Brian dances, I see what Darwin meant when he said that we were .... from apes (9).

11 I am very .... to you for all your help (8).

13 My wife is .... in French and German and also has a reasonable working knowledge of Spanish and Italian (6).

15 I'm .... of eating potatoes every day. Why can't we have rice for a change? (5)

16 Wales is .... for its male-voice choirs (6).

17 The man was found .... of the crime and sentenced to four years' imprisonment (6).

What are they saying? 1

Supply the missing preposition(s) in each caption and then match it to the appropriate cartoon.

ⓐ

1 Why can't you hide .... a newspaper .... breakfast like other husbands?

ⓑ

2 What do you mean it's not that bad? I'm standing .... my husband's shoulders!

ⓒ

3 I think we'd better apologise .... them .... waking them up.

ⓓ

4 I'm allergic .... feathers, you see.

5 You used to gaze .... me like that!

6 It's amazing .... me how people always seem to get married .... alphabetical order.

7 What do you mean you can't sleep .... the light on?

8 This is the part I don't like – having to think .... different names .... them all.

9 What a pity you haven't brought your little dog .... you. We were so looking forward .... seeing him again.

10 Do I take it you object .... my smoking a pipe?

7 Word association 1

Each of the words and phrases on the left can be associated with one of the prepositional phrases on the right. Try to match them up correctly.

1	recite a poem	a	against the law
2	We're late!	b	at daybreak
3	What a mess!	c	at the same time
4	very fashionable	d	behind schedule
5	I can't pay!	e	behind the times
6	You're too young!	f	by degrees
7	illegal	g	from memory
8	simultaneous	h	in agony
9	no clothes	i	in arrears
10	I haven't eaten!	j	behind bars
11	old-fashioned	k	in disorder
12	It really hurts!	l	in flames
13	very early	m	in the nude
14	a prisoner	n	in vogue
15	It's burning!	o	on an empty stomach
16	gradually	p	under age

Write your answers here?

1	2	3	4	5	6	7	8	9	10	11	12	13	14	15	16

8 One word only 1

Read through the following and fill in the numbered blanks with one suitable word. (Most of the missing words are prepositions.)

Travel plans

I live (1) .... Sweden, but every summer I like to travel (2) ....
Britain to visit my family and friends. I hate flying, so last summer I decided that
for a (3) .... I would travel (4) .... bus. (5) .... to the
brochure I received (6) .... the travel agency, the bus would leave Malmö
(7) .... 9.30 (8) .... Friday evening and arrive (9) ....
London the following Sunday at 7.30 (10) .... the morning. The journey
would involve taking the boat (11) .... Trelleborg on the south
(12) .... of Sweden to Travemünde (13) .... West Germany. Then
we would drive (14) .... Germany, Holland and Belgium (15) ....
taking another boat (16) .... Ostend (17) .... Dover. It sounded
wonderful – (18) .... least (19) .... theory.

In (20) ...., the journey was a nightmare from (21) .... to
finish. (22) .... begin (23) ...., I made the mistake
(24) .... not reserving a berth (25) .... Trelleborg and
Travemünde since it was quite impossible to sleep (26) .... to the
combined singing (27) .... groups of drunk Germans and Swedes, each
trying (28) .... outdo the other in (29) .... of volume and
vulgarity.

Again, I had forgotten that you are not allowed to smoke (30) ....
Swedish buses, which made the journey (31) .... stops seem even longer
than it was (32) .... reality. It also meant that when we did eventually
have a break I spent the whole time (33) .... up for the hours when I had
not been able to smoke, (34) .... the result that I could not be bothered to
waste valuable "smoking" time (35) .... queuing up (36) .... a
meal.

(37) .... the time we reached London I was a physical and mental
wreck! I had not slept or eaten properly (38) .... almost thirty-six hours
and all I wanted to do was sleep. So I booked (39) .... a really shoddy hotel
next (40) .... Victoria Coach Station and slept soundly (41) ....
twelve hours, (42) .... the same time vowing that never again would I
make the journey from Sweden (43) .... Britain by bus (44) ....
fact, (45) .... that experience, flying took (46) .... a whole new
dimension and far (47) .... hating it, I would now not dream
(48) .... travelling any other way.

Nouns following "at"

Complete the table on the right by filling in the blanks in the following sentences.

1 The car came round the corner at full ....

2 I'm not exactly sure how old he is, but at a .... I'd say about forty-five.

3 He was a very good shot and could kill an elk at a .... of 300 metres.

4 We decided to leave at .... in order to get there before midday.

5 He was very reluctant to do it at ...., but in the end he agreed.

6 Although we had not met before, my host soon made me feel completely at ....

7 Despite what people might hope, women are still at a .... when it comes to getting a top job.

8 The normal price was £25, but since I knew him, he let me have them at a ....

9 Working in a bank isn't the most exciting job in the world, perhaps, but at .... it pays the rent.

10 In Britain, it is very common to put the cat out at ....

11 Between 1939 and 1945, Britain was at .... with Germany.

12 At ...., after being turned down by ten publishers, he managed to get his novel accepted.

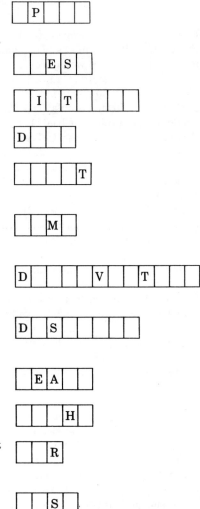

alejandro

13 I'm afraid Ms Simpson's not here at the
    .... Could you call back later?

		M		N	

14 There was a large notice in the school
    cloakroom that said: COATS ARE LEFT
    HERE AT YOUR OWN ....

R			

15 He went out to India to experience at
    first .... the Indian way of life.

	A		

Shirley wrote to her friend, Linda, giving her instructions how to reach her house. Part of the letter is reproduced below. Look at the following map and fill in the missing prepositions in Shirley's letter.

When you get (1) .... the bus, start walking (2) .... the High Street (3) .... the church. (4) .... the way, you'll pass a pub called the King's Head and a telephone kiosk. Just (5) .... the telephone kiosk, (6) .... the left, there is a car park. Go (7) .... the car park and continue (8) .... the footpath that goes (9) .... Box Wood. Turn right (10) .... the signpost and walk (11) .... the river bank until you come (12) .... a bridge. Don't go (13) .... the bridge but keep on walking until you reach a cottage called 'Hillside'. (14) .... the cottage there is a narrow road that leads (15) .... a farm. Follow the road and turn left just (16) .... reaching the farm. (17) .... the end (18) .... this road there is a row (19) .... houses. I live (20) .... the middle house. It's number 10 and has a lamp-post (21) .... it. If I'm not in, go (22) .... the back, where you'll find a spare key (23) .... the front door (24) .... the right (25) .... the back door, (26) .... a flowerpot. I hope you don't get lost!

Looking forward (27) .... seeing you again.
Lots of love,
Shirley

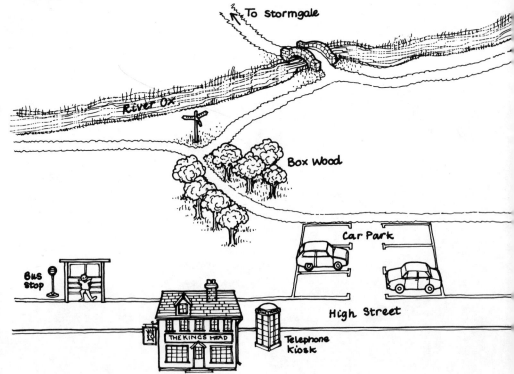

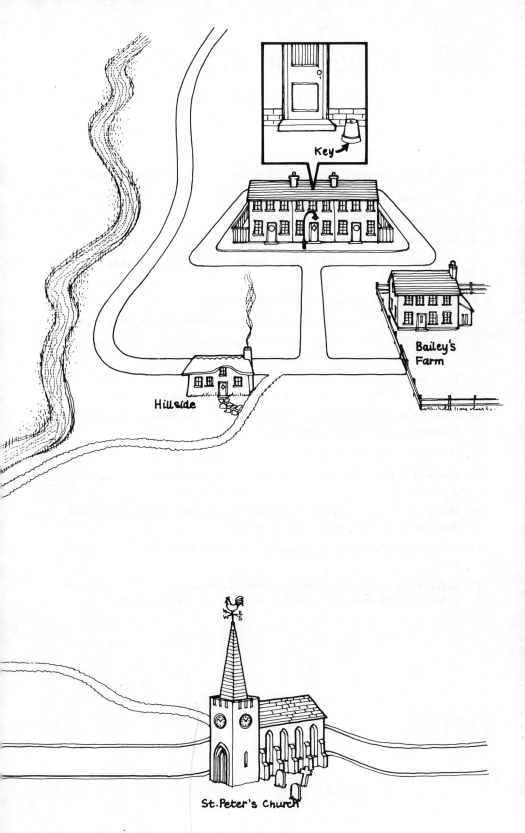

Key

Bailey's
Farm

Hillside

St. Peter's Church

11 Choose the preposition 2: at, about, against, from, of

*Complete the following sentences using **at**, **about**, **against**, **from** or **of**.*

1   I don't know her exact age; I can only guess .... how old she really is.

2   She intended to post my letter, but she forgot all .... it.

3   How does a frog differ .... a toad?

4   Tall people are definitely .... an advantage at a football match.

5   It's a pity .... poor old Fred: everyone got a Christmas present except him.

6   After the war, several people were tried for crimes .... humanity.

7   I know .... experience that I do my best work early in the morning.

8   Mrs Dale says her husband neglects her. I don't know what she's worrying .... : mine never leaves me alone.

9   I am astonished .... the way my students can spend all night at the disco and still remember their prepositions next morning.

10   On May Day, in a startling departure .... tradition, the President got on a bicycle and rode round Red Square.

11   Is it possible to insure yourself .... nuclear attack?

12   Today I feel really miserable, because I cannot find anything to complain ....

13   Resulting .... their exhaustive research into the matter, scientists can now confirm that we are all getting older.

14   I bought an old car cheaply, cleaned it up and sold it next day .... a profit.

15   Before going to Africa, Graham had himself inoculated .... tetanus, yellow fever, cholera and typhoid. A week later, he died of influenza.

16 At school today, we had a long discussion .... the best way to learn a foreign language.

17 The best reason for having strict rules at school is that it gives the pupils something to rebel .... when they are older.

18 "How can I discourage my boyfriend .... trying to kiss me all the time?"
"Eat plenty of garlic."

19 Raise the gun to your shoulder, aim .... the target, and try not to kill anyone.

20 Picking your nose in public is not illegal, but it is certainly an offence .... good manners.

12 Prepositions after adjectives 1

Complete the sentences below with one of the following adjectives plus a preposition.

addicted	bad	eligible	involved
adequate	capable	expert	jealous
angry	disqualified	full	notorious
aware	distracted	inspired	sympathetic

1   Do you think politicians are .... telling lies?

2   Don't ask me to add up the bill. I'm really .... mathematics.

3   This piece of music was .... by Beethoven's Moonlight Sonata.

4   The flat wasn't very big, but it was perfectly .... our needs.

5   Never become .... cigarettes!

6   Although he wouldn't admit it, everyone could see that he was ....
his wife's success.

7   He was .... the race for taking drugs.

8   My neighbour is .... pruning fruit trees.

9   "Who else was .... the crime?" the policeman asked the suspect.

10   He was nearly sixteen before he first became .... the opposite sex.

11   He tried to work but was .... the noise from the traffic.

12   Life is .... surprises, isn't it?

13   Pop groups are .... smashing up hotel rooms.

14   The teacher was .... her students for not doing their homework.

15   Although they said they were .... our cause, they were not prepared
to support us officially.

16   Only unmarried women are .... membership.

13 Time expressions

*The underlined expressions can be replaced by a time expression based on the word given in **CAPITAL LETTERS**. Supply the missing prepositions.*

Example: We'll grow all our own vegetables <u>in future</u>. **ON**

We'll grow all our own vegetables from <u>now on</u> .

1 Most of her clothes are no <u>longer fashionable</u>. **DATE**

2 You really make me angry <u>sometimes</u>. **TIMES**

3 I hope to see you all again <u>soon</u>. **LONG**

4 You'll have to make your own bed <u>in future</u>. **ON**

5 <u>Now and then</u> we like to spend a weekend in the mountains. **TIME**

6 Autumn is the time when fruit like apples and pears are <u>available</u>. **SEASON**

7 The demonstrators occupied the square for several hours until they were <u>eventually</u> driven away by the police. **LENGTH**

8 Wendy said that she would like to dance, and <u>immediately</u> there were twenty young men offering to dance with her. **TIME**

9 We'll be in the UK, but <u>only briefly</u>. **LONG**

10 Nobody wanted to buy his car, so <u>finally</u> he had to give it away. **END**

11 Our daughter left home three years ago, and we don't know <u>even now</u> what happened to her. **DAY**

12 Please complete the rest of your assignments <u>right away</u>. **DELAY**

13 Your Aunt Kate is using the spare bedroom <u>now</u> ... **MOMENT**

14 ... so you'll have to sleep in the garden <u>temporarily</u>. **BEING**

15 I hope to see you next month. <u>Until then</u>, best of luck with your driving test. **MEANTIME**

16 Please be very quiet. There is an examination <u>going on</u>. **PROGRESS**

14 Rewrite the sentences 1

For each of the sentences below, write a new sentence as similar as possible in meaning to the original sentence using the word in CAPITAL LETTERS. We have given you the first word(s) of the new sentence.

Example: My father has always liked football. **INTERESTED.**

My father has always been interested in football.

1 Everyone has heard about the leaning tower of Pisa. **FAMOUS**
   Pisa ....

2 This passport can be used in most countries. **VALID**
   This ....

3 They didn't tell anyone they were getting married. **SECRET**
   They ....

4 Are you and Jennifer related? **RELATIVE**
   Is ....

5 Do you want a drink? **CARE**
   Would ....

6 I lent my cousin £5. **BORROWED**
   My cousin ....

7 A car crashed into a bus this morning. **COLLIDED**
   A car ....

8 We didn't think she would pass the exam. **DOUBTFUL**
   We ....

9 He found it hard to open the window. **DIFFICULTY**
   He ....

10 Pay no attention to what she says. **NOTICE**
    Take ....

11 The painting is worth £25,000. **VALUED**
    The ....

12 She doesn't find her present job very interesting. **BORED**
    She ....

13 He was seventy-six when he died. **AGE**
He ....

14 She lived just outside the town. **OUTSKIRTS**
She ....

15 He laughed very loudly when he saw the clown. **ROARED**
He ....

16 Our customs and theirs are not the same. **DIFFERENT**
Our ....

17 I don't feel like going out tonight. **MOOD**
I ....

18 She spent the evening alone. **HERSELF**
She ....

15 It's joke time 1

Complete the following jokes by filling in the missing prepositions.

1 *Doctor*: Did you drink your orange juice .... your bath?
  Patient: .... drinking the bath, I didn't have too much room
              .... the orange juice.

2 *Teacher*: Where are you from?
  Student: Germany.
  Teacher: Which part?
  Student: All .... me.

3 *Patient*: Doctor! Doctor! I think I'm a dog.
  Doctor: Sit down, please.
  Patient: I can't. I'm not allowed .... the furniture.

4 *Teacher*: If we breathe oxygen .... the daytime, what do we breathe
              .... night?
  Student: Nitrogen?

5 *Patient*: I keep feeling I'm covered .... gold paint.
  Psychiatrist: Don't worry, that's just a gilt complex.

6 *Teacher*: James, where are the Andes?
  James: .... the end .... my armies, Miss.

7 *Hiker*: Tell me, will this path take me .... the main road?
  Local: No, sir, you'll have to go .... yourself.

8 *Teacher*: What's the definition .... 'minimum'?
  Student: A very small mother.

9 *Man*: I had to give up tap dancing.
  Woman: Why?
  Man: I kept falling .... the sink.

10 *Mother*: Brian, did you fall down .... your new trousers on?
  Brian: Yes, Mum, there wasn't time to take them off.

11 *Doctor*: Good morning, Mrs Gibbs. I haven't seen you .... a long
      time.
  Mrs Gibbs: I know, Doctor. I've been ill.

12 *Girl*: My cousin's very good .... bird impressions.
  Boy: Really?
  Girl: Yes. He eats worms!

13 *Patient*: Doctor, have you got anything .... my liver?
    Doctor: How about some onions?

14 *Man*: My neighbours bang .... the wall .... all hours.
    Friend: Doesn't that keep you awake?
    Man: No, but it really interferes .... my trumpet practice!

15 *Girl*: You remind me .... the sea.
    Boy: Because I'm so wild and romantic?
    Girl: No, you make me sick.

16 *Father*: Johnny, I've had a letter .... your headmaster. It seems you're very careless .... your appearance.
    Johnny: Am I, Dad?
    Father: Yes, you haven't appeared .... school .... last term.

Nouns following "by"

Complete the table on the right by filling in the blanks in the following sentences.

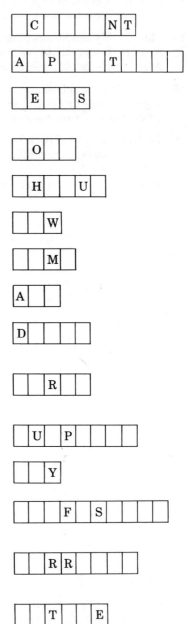

1   I didn't mean to do it; it was by ....

2   I'm sorry, but Dr Salmon sees patients by .... only.

3   By all .... bring your girlfriend with you to the party on Saturday.

4   I'd hate to go from England to Australia by .... Just imagine being seasick for six weeks!

5   He didn't have any cash, so he paid by ....

6   Hotels have to have fire escapes by ....

7   I know her by ...., but I've never actually seen her.

8   Statistically, the safest way of travelling is by ....

9   I usually buy my eggs by the ....

10 As the troublemakers wouldn't leave the disco peacefully, they had to be removed by ....

11 The announcement that the company had been taken over took all the employees by ....

12 By the ...., my name's James Samuels. I'm Miss Thompson's assistant.

13 He was a doctor by ....

14 My cousin is related to the Archbishop of Canterbury by .... Her husband is the Archbishop's brother.

15 She was a shy, retiring person by .... who hated being the centre of attention.

17 Phrasal verbs (verb + preposition)

*Rewrite the following sentences using the verb in **CAPITAL LETTERS** to replace the underlined words. You may need to rearrange the remaining words and to change the tense or the form of the verb.*

Example: Who's taking care of the children? **LOOK**

Who's looking after the children?

Choose from the following prepositions:

about	at	from	on	through	with
across	by	in	over	to	
against	for	into	round	towards	

1 I can see that my dog really likes you. **TAKE**
2 Would you like to explain in more detail what you proposed at our last meeting? **ELABORATE**
3 Michael did not hesitate to take advantage of the chance to go to Australia. **JUMP**
4 Will I be at a disadvantage because of my age? **COUNT**
5 Where were you born and brought up? **HAIL**
6 Many people are opposed to women with small children going out to work. **HOLD**
7 The repairs we have had to do on the car have really used up a lot of our savings. **EAT**
8 Tedious as it was, I had to examine a large number of documents before I found what I was looking for. **PLOUGH**
9 She happened to find the missing pearl necklace while she was looking for something else. **STUMBLE**
10 Any money I have to spare is added to the money I am saving for my holiday. **PUT**
11 Everybody deserted John after he was arrested and put on trial for embezzlement, but his wife told him: "I will not abandon you, John, whatever happens." **STICK**
12 She decided to treat herself to the luxury of a bottle of expensive champagne to celebrate her promotion. **INDULGE**
13 During the interview, the Prime Minister tried to avoid going into detail about the part of the story that he found embarrassing. **GLOSS**
14 Everyone is full of enthusiasm for Lloyd Webber's latest musical. **RAVE**
15 I am happy to confirm that he is a man of integrity. **VOUCH**
16 Little boys know how to behave in such a way that their parents will give them what they want. **GET**

18 "On time" or "in time"?

Choose the best alternative to complete each of the following sentences.

1   We arrived just (in time/on time) to see the Queen arrive at the threatre.

2   Is it true that Simon (died of/died from) cancer?

3   I was (at the point/on the point of) going out when the telephone rang.

4   Do you remember that scene (at the end/in the end) when Richard Burton and Elizabeth Taylor have a terrific argument?

5   He may seem tough and ruthless, but (by heart/at heart) he's a kind and gentle man.

6   You know you can always come to me (at the time of/in time of) need.

7   He never travelled abroad (for fear of/in fear of) becoming ill through eating foreign food.

8   Although he says he is (friendly to/friendly with) our cause, he refuses to support it openly.

9   The mother gave her three children a bar of chocolate and told them to (divide it between/divide it among) themselves.

10   These paintings have been (in possession of/in the possession of) my family for generations.

11   My cousin is very (clever at/clever with) repairing things.

12   You're so selfish! You never (care about/care for) anyone but yourself!

13   When I was a secondary school teacher, I knew all my pupils (by name/in name).

14   You're not (angry at/angry with) being kept waiting, are you?

15   I know them both (by sight/on sight), but I've no idea what their names are.

16   Who's that standing (at the front of/in front of) Julie in the photo?

17   Hands up all those (in favour of/in favour with) going to Brighton for the annual outing.

18   The proposal was accepted (on principle/in principle), but the committee asked for further details before making a final decision.

19   (In case of/In the case of) difficulty, you can reach me at this number.

20   (In view of/With a view to) the fact that only three people have signed up for Friday's concert, I'm afraid we'll have to cancel it.

19 Idiomatic prepositional phrases

Complete the sentences below with one of the following prepositions:

at	get	out of
by	in	under
from	on	up to

Some may be used more than once.

1 The boss didn't punish Kevin for coming late. He must be .... his good books.

2 He's almost dying; I'm afraid he's .... his last legs.

3 There's nothing else she can do now – the matter is completely .... her hands.

4 People told one another the news. It was passed .... word of mouth.

5 Since he won Wimbledon, everyone wants to interview him. He's .... great demand.

6 Although the police suspected him, he could prove that he was working when the crime was committed, so now he is .... the clear.

7 She's very busy at the moment; she's .... her eyes in work.

8 He came from a very poor family, so he learnt .... first hand what it was like to be hungry.

9 The police arrived just in time; they came .... the eleventh hour.

10 She rarely goes to the cinema – just once .... a blue moon.

11 They lived on only £25 a week. They lived .... a shoestring.

12 He'll never pass his exam – not .... a month of Sundays.

13 The goods were not sold openly but were available .... the counter.

14 He hasn't won yet – not .... a long chalk.

15 She never once needed to consult the manual; she had all the information .... her fingertips.

16 People arrived slowly, two or three at a time. They arrived .... dribs and drabs.

17 Stop wasting time! Get to my office .... the double.

18 I hate spiders. I get .... a cold sweat just thinking about them.

19 He's not lying. Everything he's told us so far is .... the level.

20 I know everything there is to know about Roman Britain. I know the subject .... A to Z.

Crossword 2

Read through the sentences below and complete the crossword. The missing words are either prepositions or nouns.

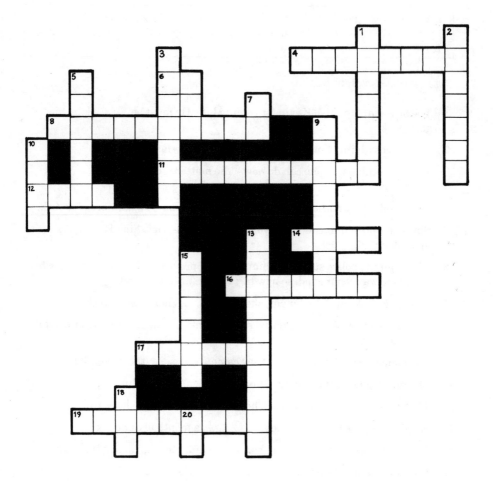

ACROSS

4 There has been a sharp .... in the number of people staying on at school over the age of sixteen. There are at least 25 per cent more now than there were three years ago (8).

6 For this job you need to be fluent in French and have a good working knowledge .... at least two other European languages (2).

8 Germans have a .... for being very efficient and hard-working (10).

11 You shouldn't have any .... in getting to know people in Greece. Everyone is so friendly there (10).

12 Being tall, she had a certain advantage .... others in the team (4).

14 In some countries, companies are not allowed to do business .... South Africa (4).

16 Fighting the threat of pollution is a race .... time (7).

17 Can I have the .... for your fruit cake? (6)

19 'To be or not to be' is a famous .... from *Hamlet* (9).

DOWN

1 RSPCA stands for the Royal Society for the Prevention of .... to Animals (7).

2 Is there a great difference .... British and American English? (7)

3 What is your attitude .... foreigners? (7)

5 On his eighteenth birthday his grandfather gave him a .... for £1,000 (6).

7 Brazil is rich .... natural resources (2).

9 Does anyone have a .... to the problem? (8)

10 The verdict was death .... natural causes (4).

13 I've just heard of Tom's .... to Angela. I wonder when the wedding will be? (10)

15 Since he was a mechanic, I asked for his .... on buying a second-hand car (6).

18 Is your wife still having treatment .... asthma? (3)

20 She is heir .... the family fortune. That's probably why so many men would like to marry her (2).

The two letters below are all mixed up. Try to sort them out. Mark the first letter 1–9 and the second one a–k. (The first part of Letter 1 has been done for you.)

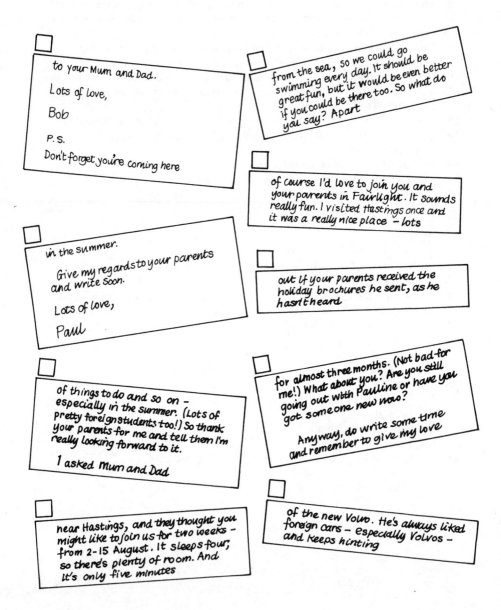

to your Mum and Dad.

Lots of love,

Bob

P.S.

Don't forget you're coming here

---

from the sea, so we could go swimming every day. It should be great fun, but it would be even better if you could be there too. So what do you say? Apart

---

of course I'd love to join you and your parents in Fairlight. It sounds really fun. I visited Hastings once and it was a really nice place – lots

---

in the summer.

Give my regards to your parents and write soon.

Lots of love,

Paul

---

out if your parents received the holiday brochures he sent, as he hasn't heard

---

of things to do and so on – especially in the summer. (Lots of pretty foreign students too!) So thank your parents for me and tell them I'm really looking forward to it.

I asked Mum and Dad

---

for almost three months. (Not bad for me!) What about you? Are you still going out with Pauline or have you got someone new now?

Anyway, do write some time and remember to give my love

---

near Hastings, and they thought you might like to join us for two weeks – from 2-15 August. It sleeps four, so there's plenty of room. And it's only five minutes

---

of the new Volvo. He's always liked foreign cars – especially Volvos – and keeps hinting

☐ for my birthday party on the nineteenth. (Bring Pauline, if you like!)

☐ With exams and everything, so I hope you understand.

My main reason for writing, however is to ask if you feel like spending a couple of weeks with us

☐ from them yet.

Well, Bob, that's all for now. I hope you're keeping well and that you'll be able to join us

☐ Dear Paul,

Many thanks for your letter. It was nice to hear from you at last. (I was beginning to think you'd emigrated!)

About the summer, yes

☐ With Sally. You remember Sally, don't you? She was the girl I met at Jenny's birthday party. We've been together now

☐ for all the trouble he's gone to.

By the way, Paul, Dad's very jealous

☐ in the summer? Mum and Dad have hired a caravan in Fairlight – a little village

☐ to Mum about getting a new car. But she's not interested really, so I don't think he'll persuade her.

Well, Paul, I'll stop now because I'm off to a disco

1 Dear Bob,

Sorry I've taken such a long time in answering your letter, but the truth is that I've been really busy these past few weeks

☐ about the holiday brochures and they say they haven't received them yet. (Well, you know what the post is like!) But they'll write as soon as they get them, and they asked me to tell you to thank your Dad

☐ from this, there's not much else to say really. Dad's got a new car – a Volvo – and Mum's just started back to work again.

By the way, Dad asked me to find

22 Compound prepositions 1

Complete the prepositional phrases below by choosing a word from the following list. When you have finished, try to make up a sentence using each of the phrases.

a cost	good terms	the accompaniment
agreement	means	the benefit
aid	peace	the compliments
answer	pity	the influence
behalf	reference	work
compensation		

1   at .... on

2   at .... of

3   at .... with

4   by .... of

5   for .... of

6   in .... of

7   in .... with

8   in .... to

9   in .... for

10   on .... of

11   on .... with

12   out of .... for

13   to .... of

14   under .... of

15   with .... to

16   with .... of

23 Choose the preposition 3: in, into, on, over

*Complete the following sentences using **in**, **into**, **on** or **over**.*

1 Do you take pride .... your appearance, or are you just vain?

2 I tripped .... the cat and fell downstairs.

3 The film *The Magnificent Seven* was based .... a Japanese story about the samurai.

4 Don't kiss the Prince, or he might change .... a frog.

5 If you can't finish the report by Friday, please try to get it done .... the weekend.

6 Father must be .... a bad temper: he has just thrown mother out of the window.

7 All forms of travel are expensive nowadays, but, ... balance, air travel offers the best value for money.

8 Extensive research .... artificial sweeteners has shown that rats die quickly if you drop large blocks of saccharin on them.

9 There seems to be some confusion .... what Nelson actually said as he lay dying: Was it "Kiss me, Hardy" or "Kismet, Hardy"?

10 There has been a considerable improvement .... the flow of traffic since they opened the extra lanes on the M25.

11 There's no point in getting upset .... things that are beyond your control.

12 The only way to prevent children from getting .... trouble is to keep them locked up until they are twenty-one.

13 The party's new policy document puts a strong emphasis .... public ownership of basic utilities like electricity and water.

14 I am a bit weak .... science subjects, but I am trying to improve.

15 If you put as much effort .... your studies as you do .... football, you might have a chance.

16 I've been .... your essay, and I wore out three red pens making corrections.

17 Is it true that Peter is currently engaged .... writing a book about Swedish humour?

18 Do you pride yourself .... looking smart, or are you simply trying to impress me?

19 Make yourself a drink while I go and slip .... something more comfortable.

20 The last item .... the agenda is "Any Other Business".

alejandro Gómez Pesco

24 Nouns following "in" 1

Complete the table on the right by filling in the blanks in the following sentences.

1 The most popular game in England in the .... is cricket.

	U		E	

2 This car may be old, but it's still in very good ....

		D	T			

3 Keep away from Simon; he's in a really bad .... this morning.

	O		

4 I can't stop, I'm afraid. I'm in a ....

			Y	

5 All school fees must be paid in ....

	V		C	

6 In an .... dial 999.

M		R			Y

7 That joke was in very bad ...., Colin. You should be ashamed of yourself.

T				

8 You'd better take some extra money with you in .... you need to take a taxi home.

	A		

9 During the Second World War, most messages were sent in ....

	D		

10 What I'm about to tell you is in .... So please don't say anything to anyone else.

C		F				C

11 The secret service tried to warn the President that his life would be in .... if he carried out his plan to visit South Africa.

		G		R	

12 I'm afraid the bank can't lend you more money, Mrs Jarvis, You're already over £800 in ....

	B		

13 I always stay in .... until 12 o'clock on Sundays.

E		

14 In ...., may I say how grateful I am to everyone for making today such a big success.

O		L			N

15 There's nothing wrong with drinking alcohol as long as it's done in ....

	D	R	T		

25 Rewrite the sentences 2

For each of the sentences below, write a new sentence as similar as possible in meaning to the original sentence using the word in **CAPITAL LETTERS**. *We have given you the first word(s) of the new sentence.*

Example: My father has always liked football. **INTERESTED**

My father has always been <u>interested</u> in football.

1 Your car is just like one I used to own. **SIMILAR**
 I ....

2 He would never tell you a lie. **INCAPABLE**
 He ....

3 When Mary was pregnant, all she wanted to eat was jelly. **CRAVING**
 Mary ....

4 My boss seems to enjoy humiliating people. **PLEASURE**
 My boss ....

5 I don't usually speak to strange men. **HABIT**
 I ....

6 The interview panel thought that Sarah had a very good manner. **IMPRESSION**
 Sarah ....

7 If you want to understand Yeats's poetry, you need to study Irish history. **KEY**
 Irish history ....

8 Sports cars are John's great passion. **CRAZY**
 John ....

9 All my friends have left me. **DESERTED**
 I ....

10 My best friend is someone I can really trust. **CONFIDENCE**
 I ....

11 Henry really knew how to make people laugh. **TALENT**
 Henry ....

12 My father says that the moon is made of green cheese. **ACCORDING**
 The moon ....

13 The people of Dolichorrhinia are noted for their long noses. **CHARACTERISTIC**
 Long noses ....

14 I can recite the whole of Wordsworth's *Prelude* without looking at the book. **MEMORY**
 I ....

15 We have run out of the items you want. **STOCK**
 The items ....

16 It was very kind of you to help me. **GRATEFUL**
 I ....

17 The way to get the best out of me is to make me work very hard. **PRESSURE**
 I ....

18 All the teachers like Kate. **POPULAR**
 Kate ....

26 Prepositions after verbs 1

Complete the sentences below with one of the following verbs plus a preposition. (Make any changes to verb tenses that may be necessary.)

apologise	correspond	hear	pray
arrive	die	knock	rhyme
belong	distinguish	leave	suffer
complain	experiment	lose	vote

1   Did you .... Tom and Sally? They've decided to emigrate to New Zealand.

2   If you don't agree with the proposal, you can always .... it at the meeting.

3   It was almost midnight when we .... the station.

4   Some people find it difficult to .... an American and a Canadian.

5   The priest said he would .... us.

6   Although he had survived the battle, the soldier later .... his wounds.

7   For years, his wife had .... varicose veins.

8   Do you think people should be allowed to .... animals?

9   I don't know why, but I really hate .... cards. It puts me in a bad mood all day.

10   He .... the manager about the poor service at the restaurant.

11   Would you say that the British House of Lords .... the American Senate?

12   Do you know who this book ....?

13   Can you think of a word that .... "numb"?

14   I think there's someone .... the door.

15   He .... the organisers for his bad behaviour at the conference.

16   We .... Paris next week. We'll probably stay there for a fortnight.

27 Phrasal verbs + preposition

Complete each of the sentences using one of these adverb + preposition pairs:

around to	back on	in for	over to
around for	behind with	in with	up on
away for	down to	on at	up to
away with	down with	out for	up with

1   Did you get this booklet from a bookshop?
No, I had to write .... it.

2   Is Pat ill again? She's forever going .... some illness or other!

3   Just because I kissed you last night, don't run .... the idea that I am serious about you.

4   An outgoing Chairman always hands .... his successor at the end of the Annual General Meeting.

5   He thinks he's superior to everyone else. That's why he always talks .... people.

6   If you go into the park alone at night, watch .... muggers.

7   I've had so many other things to do lately that I've fallen .... my studies. Never mind, I'll soon catch up.

8   "When are you going to mend that broken window?"
"Don't worry, I'll get .... it one of these days."

9   I was very disappointed when I went to see Rod Stewart in concert. He certainly failed to live .... my expectations.

10   When the sky is red in the morning, it means we are .... some bad weather.

11   I've been looking .... somewhere to live, but I haven't found anything suitable so far.

12   When money is short, you have to think about cutting .... luxuries.

13   I didn't bring any money with me. If you'll pay for the meal, I'll settle .... you later.

14   My parents nag me constantly. They keep .... me to smarten myself up and get a proper job.

15   If you're going to apply for that interpreter's job, you'd better brush .... your French and German.

16   "When shall we meet for lunch?"
"Well, I'm free any time, so I'll fit .... your plans."

28 One word only 2

Read through the following and fill in the numbered blanks with a suitable preposition. Be careful, however, in some cases there may be more than one alternative; in others, no preposition is needed.

It was a very happy funeral. Even the sun shone that day (1) .... the late Henry Ground. Lying (2) .... his coffin, he was probably enjoying himself too. Once more, and (3) .... the last time (4) .... this earth, he was the centre (5) .... attention. People laughed and told (6) .... each other jokes. Relatives who had not spoken (7) .... years smiled (8) .... each other and promised to stay (9) .... touch (10) .... now on. And, (11) .... course, everyone had a favourite story to tell (12) .... Henry.

"What (13) .... the time he dressed up (14) .... gypsy costume and went (15) .... door (16) .... door telling people's fortunes? He actually made £6 (17) .... an afternoon!"

"That reminds me (18) .... the time I was having dinner (19) .... him (20) .... a posh restaurant. When the wine waiter brought the wine, he poured a drop (21) .... Henry's glass and waited (22) .... a superior expression (23) .... his face. So Henry, instead (24) .... tasting (25) .... it, the way any normal person would, dipped his thumb and forefinger (26) .... the wine (27) .... his glass. Then he put his hand (28) .... his ear and rolled his forefinger and thumb together as if he were *listening* (29) .... the quality (30) .... the wine! Then he nodded (31) .... the waiter solemnly, as if to say 'Yes, that's fine. You may serve it.' You should have seen the look (32) .... the wine waiter's face! And how Henry managed to keep (33) .... laughing, I'll never know!"

"Did you hear (34) .... the practical joke he played when he was a student (35) .... Oxford, the one (36) .... the roadmenders. Some workmen were digging a hole (37) .... the road. First, Henry went (38) .... the police and told (39) .... them (40) .... some 'students' who were digging the road up (41) .... a joke. Then he approached (42) .... the workmen, and explained (43) .... them that some students had dressed up as policemen and were coming to tell them to stop digging the hole! Well, you can imagine what happened!"

"Yes, old Henry loved to play tricks (44) .... people. Once, when he was invited (45) .... a modern art exhibition, he managed somehow to get (46) .... the gallery the day before and turn all the paintings upside down. The exhibition ran (47) .... four days before anyone noticed!"

"It's hard to believe that Henry was a Ground, when you think how different he was (48) .... his brothers."

Yes, it was difficult to believe (49) .... that he was a Ground. He was born (50) .... an unimportant but well-to-do family (51) .... the Midlands. He was the youngest (52) .... five sons. The four older boys were all successful (53) .... life. They married beautiful girls (54) .... good family, and produced children as handsome and clever as themselves. The eldest son became a clergyman; the second was appointed (55) .... headmaster (56) .... a famous public school; the third went (57) .... business and became disgustingly rich; the fourth followed (58) .... his father's footsteps and became a solicitor. But the youngest Ground, Henry, (59) .... his brothers, turned out to be a lazy good- (60) ....-nothing. (61) .... Henry, an energetic afternoon consisted (62) .... sitting (63) .... a shady tree, (64) .... a pretty companion (65) .... his side, and all the time (66) .... the world to learn the songs (67) .... the bees that buzzed (68) .... his head.

Some people whispered that his real father was not the respectable Mr Ground (69) .... all, but a wild gypsy who had come one day (70) .... the house and had swept Mrs Ground (71) .... her feet (72) .... his dancing black eyes and his wicked country ways.

(Adapted from the story "The Joker" in *The Penguin Book of Very Short Stories*.)

Complete the sentences below with one of the following nouns plus a preposition.

basis	cruelty	genius	objection
campaign	excuse	grudge	opposite
choice	fall	knowledge	strain
control	freedom	news	trouble

1 If you had a .... marrying for love or marrying for money, which would you do?

2 What is the .... "timid"? Is it "bold" or "brave"?

3 The African elephant will be extinct within twenty years if an international .... the ivory trade is not started immediately.

4 Do you have any .... my parking my car in front of your house?

5 The .... chewing gum is that it loses its flavour too quickly.

6 I know you have a cold, but that's no .... not doing your homework.

7 If you have to deal with overseas clients, a .... foreign languages is very useful.

8 Perhaps the three most important human rights are .... hunger, fear and persecution.

9 In our class, we can do as we like: our teacher has no .... us at all.

10 The RSPCA is concerned with prevention of .... animals.

11 Overweight people should not jog, because it puts a great .... their hearts.

12 Since the salmonella scare there has been a considerable .... the consumption of eggs.

13 Einstein was a real .... mathematics, but he couldn't add two and two together correctly!

14 In the dispute between the union and the management, new proposals have been put forward that should at least provide a .... discussion.

15 Vandalising public property is the only way some youngsters can express their .... society.

16 "Did you know that short people don't live as long as tall people?"
"No, I didn't. It's .... me!"

30 Crossword 3

*Read through the sentences below and complete the crossword. The
missing words are either verbs (in various tenses) or prepositions.*

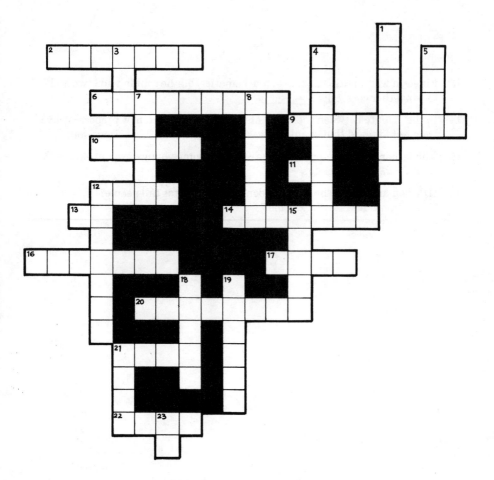

ACROSS

2   David's a bit odd, isn't he? He actually .... rain to sunshine (7).
6   We .... to Australia by boat (9).
9   Stop .... at me! I'm not deaf, you know (8).
10   She shared her birthday cake .... her friends (5).
11   We congratulated her .... passing her driving test (2).
12   The driver lost control of the car and crashed .... a lamp-post (4).
13   My grandfather died .... a train accident before I was born (2).
14   Both the candidates were so well qualified that it was very difficult to choose .... them (7).
16   If you don't agree with the verdict of the court, you can always appeal .... it (7).
17   He was discharged .... the army because of ill-health (4).
20   "What do you get if you .... 14 by 12?" "168" (8).
21   Charles must be very religious. He's always quoting passages .... the Bible (4).
22   My cousin loves writing letters. In fact he corresponds .... people all over the world (4).

DOWN

1   We went under the bridge to .... from the rain (7).
3   One of Andrew Lloyd Webber's most famous songs is "Don't Cry .... Me, Argentina" (3).
4   If it's too small, you can always go back to the shop and .... it for a larger one (8).
5   We tried to get everyone to .... in the dancing (4).
7   It doesn't matter which country you visit, people there always seem to complain .... the lack of good programmes on television (5).
8   Very few prisoners ever managed to .... from Devil's Island (6).
12   Has Michael .... you to his party on Saturday? (7)
15   You needn't .... about Bob. He'll be all right. He knows how to take care of himself (5).
18   Don't try to .... me for the accident! I wasn't even here when it happened (5).
19   She was very shy and didn't like .... with people, especially strangers (6).
21   Does the River Thames .... into the North Sea or the English Channel? (4)
23   The judge sentenced him .... six months' imprisonment (2).

Prepositions after verbs 2

Below are thirty-five verbs arranged alphabetically. Place each one of them under the correct preposition (five under each). When you have finished, see if you can make up sentences containing each of the verbs plus prepositions.

abstain	consist	expel	quarrel
appeal	cope	flee	rely
approve	decrease	glance	respond
believe	dedicate	hint	subscribe
benefit	delight	indulge	sympathise
bet	depart	invest	take advantage
coincide	depend	marvel	tread
collaborate	dispose	object	wink
concentrate	dream	point	

AT

_____
_____
_____
_____
_____

OF

_____
_____
_____
_____
_____

TO

_____
_____
_____
_____
_____

FROM

_____
_____
_____
_____
_____

ON

_____
_____
_____
_____
_____

WITH

_____
_____
_____
_____
_____

IN

_____
_____
_____
_____
_____

32 Choose the preposition 4: in, out of, to, under, with

*Complete the following sentences using **in, out of, to, under,** or **with**.*

1 .... luck, we should be in London by 3 o'clock.

2 Would you like to contribute .... our campaign fund?

3 It's not like John to lose his temper. It's completely .... character.

4 "You are .... arrest, sir."
"On what charge?"
"I'll think of something, sir."

5 The match resulted .... a goalless draw after extra time.

6 With increasing competition from overseas, several factories are threatened .... closure.

7 The talks broke down when the Cubans decided to pull .... negotiations and go home.

8 "Are all the preparations made?"
"Don't worry, everything is .... hand."

9 You look really .... the weather. Are you ill?

10 I told her .... her face exactly what I thought of her.

11 Christopher has started to take an interest .... girls, much to his father's relief.

12 We have a good working relationship .... the local authority.

13 The proposal to introduce a local income tax is still .... discussion.

14 The car went over the brow of the hill and was soon .... sight.

15 I was .... the impression that you had to be twenty-one to vote in general elections.

16 My neighbour's garage, which is adjacent .... my house, is full of rubbish.

17 This is supposed to be a socialist country, but it is socialist .... name only.

18 What it amounts .... is this: the word "socialist" means what the government want it to mean.

19 "Why have you got a pet African buffalo in the house?"
"I wanted something a little .... the ordinary."

20 Are you familiar .... Professor Wilhelm's work on bilingualism in parrots?

33 Nouns following "in" 2

Complete the table on the right by filling in the blanks in the following sentences.

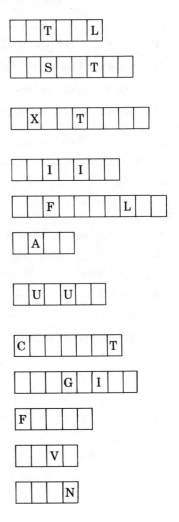

1 The detective asked the witness to describe the scene of the crime in ....

2 My mother is in .... at the moment with a broken leg.

3 This is the only known copy of the book in .... All the others were destroyed in a fire.

4 In my ...., *Fawlty Towers* with John Cleese was the funniest television comedy series ever made.

5 He told us that if we were ever in ...., we could rely on him for help.

6 I don't dislike classical music at all. In ...., I often go to the opera.

7 "I'll overlook it this time," said the teacher. "But remember to do your homework in ...."

8 Winning £2 million on the football pools made it possible for him to live in .... for the rest of his life.

9 He didn't want anyone to recognise him, so he went to the party in ....

10 Are you sure the projector's in ....? Everything looks very blurred to me.

11 Pam can't concentrate on anything these days. She's in .... again, I'm afraid.

12 Although the soldier was obviously in great ...., he never once complained.

13 Ask your solicitor if you're in .... about anything in the contract.

	U		T

14 I see that long hair is in .... again.

	A		H		

15 In ...., women are more sensitive than men.

G			R		

Sunthoms Holidays have received two letters of complaint. Unfortunately, they are mixed up. Try to sort them out. Mark the first letter 1–13 and the second one a–m. (The first part of Letter 1 has been done for you.)

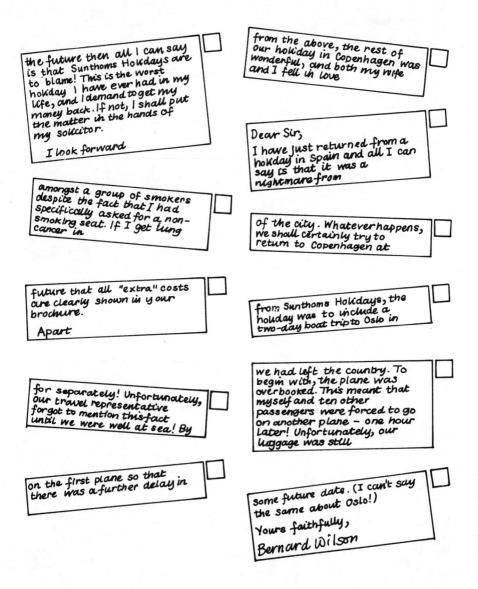

the future then all I can say is that Sunthoms Holidays are to blame! This is the worst holiday I have ever had in my life, and I demand to get my money back. If not, I shall put the matter in the hands of my solicitor.

I look forward

amongst a group of smokers despite the fact that I had specifically asked for a non-smoking seat. If I get lung cancer in

future that all "extra" costs are clearly shown in your brochure.

Apart

for separately! Unfortunately, our travel representative forgot to mention this fact until we were well at sea! By

on the first plane so that there was a further delay in

from the above, the rest of our holiday in Copenhagen was wonderful, and both my wife and I fell in love

Dear Sir,
I have just returned from a holiday in Spain and all I can say is that it was a nightmare from

of the city. Whatever happens, we shall certainly try to return to Copenhagen at

from Sunthoms Holidays, the holiday was to include a two-day boat trip to Oslo in

we had left the country. To begin with, the plane was overbooked. This meant that myself and ten other passengers were forced to go on another plane – one hour later! Unfortunately, our luggage was still

some future date. (I can't say the same about Oslo!)
Yours faithfully,
Bernard Wilson

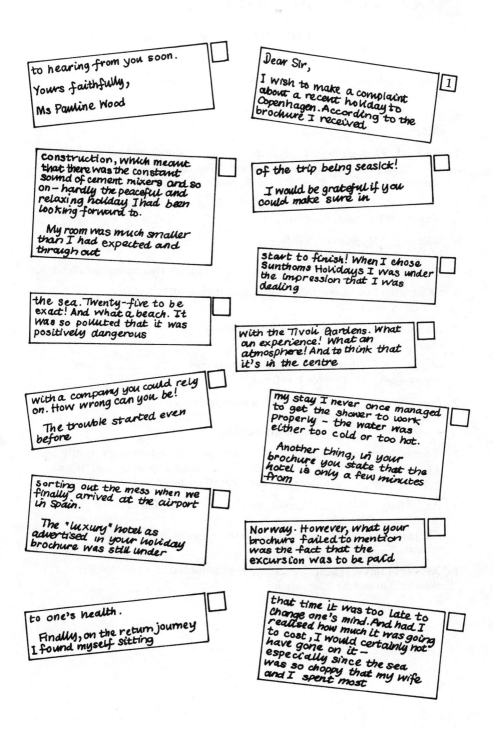

to hearing from you soon.

Yours faithfully,

Ms Pauline Wood

Dear Sir,

I wish to make a complaint about a recent holiday to Copenhagen. According to the brochure I received

1

---

construction, which meant that there was the constant sound of cement mixers and so on — hardly the peaceful and relaxing holiday I had been looking forward to.

My room was much smaller than I had expected and throughout

---

of the trip being seasick!

I would be grateful if you could make sure in

---

the sea. Twenty-five to be exact! And what a beach. It was so polluted that it was positively dangerous

---

start to finish! When I chose Sunthoms Holidays I was under the impression that I was dealing

---

with a company you could rely on. How wrong can you be!

The trouble started even before

With the Tivoli Gardens. What an experience! What an atmosphere! And to think that it's in the centre

---

sorting out the mess when we finally arrived at the airport in Spain.

The "luxury" hotel as advertised in your holiday brochure was still under

---

my stay I never once managed to get the shower to work properly — the water was either too cold or too hot.

Another thing, in your brochure you state that the hotel is only a few minutes from

---

to one's health.

Finally, on the return journey I found myself sitting

Norway. However, what your brochure failed to mention was the fact that the excursion was to be paid

---

that time it was too late to change one's mind. And had I realised how much it was going to cost, I would certainly not have gone on it — especially since the sea was so choppy that my wife and I spent most

35 It's joke time 2

Complete the following jokes by filling in the missing prepositions.

1. I've always believed .... love .... first sight ever since I looked .... a mirror.

2. BULLDOG .... SALE: Will eat anything – very fond .... children.

3. The mother kangaroo suddenly leapt .... the air and gave a cry .... pain. "Sidney!" she screamed. "How many times do I have to tell you that you cannot smoke .... bed!"

4. *Man 1*: How dare you swear .... front .... my wife!
   Man 2: Why – was it her turn?

5. *Woman 1*: My husband's career is .... ruins.
   Woman 2: Oh, I am sorry to hear that.
   Woman 1: There's nothing wrong .... that. He's an archaeologist.

6. "What's the fastest vegetable .... the world?"
   "A runner bean."

7. A sadist is someone who would put a drawing-pin .... an electric chair.

8. *Man*: What's the best way to remove paint .... a chair?
   Shopkeeper: Sit down on it before it's dry.

9. *Piano tuner*: I've come here to tune your piano.
   Man: But we didn't send .... you.
   Piano tuner: No, but your neighbours did.

10. A teenage girl sat .... a train chewing gum and staring vacantly .... space, when suddenly an old man sitting opposite said, "It's no good talking .... me, my dear, I'm stone deaf!"

11. An old lady went .... the optician's and said: "I need a new pair .... glasses."
    The optician replied: "I knew that as soon as you walked .... the window."

12. *James*: I throw myself .... everything I do.
    Susan: Go and dig a large hole!

13 *Jill*:   You're wearing your wedding ring .... the wrong finger.
   Pam: I know. I married the wrong man.

14 *Customer*:   Chemist, I'd like some poison .... mice.
   Chemist: Have you tried Boots?[1]
   Customer: I want to poison them – not kick them .... death!

15 If Superman's so intelligent, why does he wear his underpants ....
his trousers?

16 *Mark*:   I understand that the sports and social club is looking ....
   a treasurer.
   Geoffrey: That's right.
   Mark: But I thought they hired a treasurer only a few months ago.
   Geoffrey: They did. That's the treasurer they're looking ....!

[1] A chain of chemists in Britain.

36 Headlines

The prepositional verbs in these headlines each contain a one-letter spelling mistake, e.g., HOME SECRETARY TO <u>B</u>OOK INTO PRISON CONDITIONS, *which should be* HOME SECRETARY TO <u>L</u>OOK INTO PRISON CONDITIONS. *To help you find the mistakes, here is a checklist of the wrong and right letters (given in alphabetical order):*

The wrong letters: A C D E F G L L M P P R S T V

The right letters: C C D E F G J L P P P R R R Y

1   AGRICULTURE MINISTER DRESSED ON PIGS

2   FIREMEN WARNED: DON'T PUMP TO CONCLUSIONS

3   CHICKEN BREEDER ON FRAUD CHARGE TOLD BY JUDGE: "YOU WILL HAVE TO LAY HEAVILY FOR YOUR CRIMES"

4   FINANCIAL CRISIS IN SOCIAL DEMOCRAT PARTY: LEADER FALLS ON PARTY FAITHFUL TO COME TO THE RESCUE

5   NEGOTIATIONS BETWEEN MISSIONARIES AND CANNIBAL CHIEF BREAK DOWN. "IT'S IMPOSSIBLE TO SEASON WITH THEM," SAYS CHIEF

6   VETERINARY SURGEON ACCUSED OF CRUELTY TO CATS PROTESTS: "PEOPLE LIKE TO PUSS OVER NOTHING"

7   GAMBLER CONVICTED OF MURDERING BOOKMAKER BETS FOR MERCY

8   DIRECTOR OF BLOOD BANK ON CORRUPTION CHARGE IS ACCUSED OF CONGEALING EVIDENCE FROM THE POLICE

9   PREACHER WARNS: "THOSE WHO LIVE BY THE SWORD SHALL PARISH BY THE SWORD"

10 GREENGROCER TOLD TO RESTORE SIXTEENTH-CENTURY SHOP FRONT WILL APPLE TO COUNCIL FOR A GRANT

11 HIGH-SPENDING LOCAL AUTHORITIES TOLD: "MONEY DOESN'T GLOW ON TREES"

12 CLERGYMEN FROCK TO WEMBLEY TO HEAR WORLD-FAMOUS PREACHER

13 THE RICH AND THE POOR: MEN WELL-OFF, BUT WOMEN "STILL NOT SHAVING IN NATION'S WEALTH"

14 WELFARE OFFICIALS ACCUSED OF CRYING INTO COUPLES' PRIVATE LIVES

15 NEANDERTHAL MAN MATES FROM PREHISTORIC TIMES, SCIENTIST CLAIMS

37 Compound prepositions 2

Complete the prepositional phrases below by choosing a word from the following list. When you have finished, try to make up a sentence using each of the phrases.

account	exchange	regard	the expense
addition	favour	respect	the sake
common	odds	the exception	virtue

1 in .... for

2 in .... with

3 in .... to

4 in .... of

5 at .... with

6 at .... of

7 with .... to

8 with .... of

9 for .... of

10 out of .... for

11 on .... of

12 by .... of

What are they saying?   2

Supply the missing preposition(s) in each caption and then match it to the appropriate cartoon.

1 So much ....
"enriched ....
vitamins and energy-giving
minerals"!

2 Are you related ....
the Smiths ....
rooms 102, 110, 120, 130 and
141 .... any chance?

3 Sorry – we don't
have a menu. Just point
.... something
.... my apron.

4 Arthur's always been very
sensitive .... his
bald spot.

5 Actually, this is number 13. Number 14 is just .... the corner.

6 I've decided .... becoming a doctor – you have to wash your hands too often.

7 Living .... the past again, Harold?

8 I'm not .... my best first thing .... the morning.

9 Is the banging .... the wall keeping you awake, darling?

10 And, ... all, madam, my party believes .... total honesty .... politics.

39 Prepositions after adjectives 2

Complete the sentences below with one of the following adjectives plus a preposition.

accompanied	deep	faced	quick
ahead	descended	famous	sensitive
allergic	envious	fortunate	surprised
clever	exempt	peculiar	worthy

1 I was not very bright as a child, but I was so .... my hands that I decided to become a pickpocket.

2 Some plants are so .... pollution that they can only survive in a perfectly clean environment.

3 I am .... anyone who can play a musical instrument really well.

4 Sarah was very .... figures, so she eventually became a successful accountant.

5 For dinner we had grilled plaice and new potatoes, ... a splendid bottle of Chablis.

6 Newton was so .... thought that morning that he absent-mindedly put the egg in his pocket and dropped his watch into the boiling water.

7 The town of San Gimignano is .... its medieval towers.

8 Marsupials – animals that carry their young in a pouch – are .... the Antipodes.

9 My wife loves cats. She has six. I am .... them, so I sneeze whenever I am near her.

10 Janet! I'm .... you: eating chocolates when you're supposed to be slimming!

11 It is the ambition of every writer to complete a book .... schedule. So far, no one has achieved this.

12 According to Buradan, a perfectly logical donkey, ... two identical and equidistant piles of food, would starve to death, because it would have no logical reason for choosing one rather than the other.

13 Charles is disabled, so he is .... having a wife who is a trained nurse.

14 Darwin's theory suggests that we are all .... an ape-like creature, which seems likely in the case of my Aunt Matilda.

15 Candidates with university degrees are .... Parts 1 and 2 of the examination.

16 That remark was not .... you.

40 Fractured newspaper article

Can you reassemble the mixed-up pieces below to get the original newspaper article? The article begins with the words:

Dr Roy Williams, a specialist in

1 all, women should realise that going

2 women's problems, says that women are far more prone to

3 from her partner will do her the world of good."

4 the dynamic businesswoman who finds it difficult to cope. Talking about the increasing consumption of alcohol by women, Dr Williams says: "First of

5 to men to help relieve the pressure

6 whatever reason, the extra responsibility of running the house will only add

7 stress than men. His claims are backed up

8 to her troubles. A helping hand

9 for a drink after work is not the answer. It's very dangerous, especially as most women are far less tolerant

10 outside, many appear to be highly successful, but in

11 on their over-stressed partners. He says: "I've done a lot of tests on men and women over

12 by new research that reveals that career women, particularly those aged between

13 risk in today's high-stress society. On the

14 twenty-six and forty-six, are more likely to suffer

15 reality, they are anxious and depressed. If a woman is feeling down for

16 the past year, and they confirm that career women are more and more at

17 from stress than their partners. The image of the typical stress victim as a middle-aged businessman has been replaced by

18 to alcohol than men." Dr Williams believes that it is up

41 Rewrite the sentences 3

For each of the sentences below write a new sentence as similar as possible in meaning to the original sentence using the word in **CAPITAL LETTERS.** *We have given you the first word(s) of the new sentence.*

Example: My father has always liked football. **INTERESTED**

My father has always been <u>interested</u> in football.

1 People's race, creed or colour is not taken into account when they apply for a job with us. **IRRESPECTIVE**
Anyone ....

2 Many film-makers were very much influenced by *Citizen Kane*. **IMPACT**
The film ....

3 It is only a short walk from my house to the station. **HANDY**
My house ....

4 We may have to increase our prices without warning. **SUBJECT**
Our prices ....

5 Section Six of the Health and Safety Act forbids smoking in restaurant kitchens. **CONTRARY**
Smoking ....

6 She shot the intruder but only to protect herself. **SELF-DEFENCE**
She ....

7 The library has lost a number of books lately. **MISSING**
A number ....

8 I did not like the way you spoke to your sister. **DISGUSTED**
I ....

9 This rule has no exceptions. **EXCEPTIONS**
There are ....

10 Do you know the works of the poet William McGonagall? **ACQUAINTED**
Are ....

11 A lot more people are buying automatic cars these days. **DEMAND**
There ....

12 Lloyds the Butcher's and Lloyds Bank are two completely separate organisations. **CONNECTION**
Lloyds Bank ....

13 We have scarcely enough money to live on. **SHORT**

We ....

14 Pest species are excluded from the provisions of the Wildlife Protection Act. **APPLY**

The provisions ....

15 John knows a great deal about organic farming. **EXPERT**

John ....

16 We ran into a barn to get out of the rain. **SHELTER**

We ....

17 My bank manager and I get on together very well. **GOOD TERMS**

I ....

18 You and I have exactly the same pearl earrings. **IDENTICAL**

Your pearl earrings ....

42 Choose the preposition 5: after, at, in, on

*Complete the following sentences using **after, at, in** or **on**.*

1 "Who destroyed the Temple in Jerusalem?"
   "I don't know, sir, but I expect that they will blame it .... me."

2 When the offer of a free trip to Holland was made, John was very quick
   .... the mark, and managed to get the first ticket.

3 Most people would jump .... the chance to spend a year in America,
   all expenses paid.

4 When Robin told me about his quarrel with Batman, I asked him not to
   involve me .... his personal affairs.

5 Was the Clifton Suspension Bridge named .... a man called Clifton
   Suspension?

6 If trains always leave .... schedule, why do so many of them arrive
   late at the other end?

7 The survivors of the *Titanic* were .... sea for several days before
   being rescued.

8 My husband brought me some flowers today. He must be ....
   something!

9 We were all very excited .... the prospect of a free trip to Paris.

10 Does it matter what a national politician does .... private as long as
   he performs well in his job?

11 Susan is disabled but she likes to do things for herself: she hates to be
   dependent .... other people.

12 .... careful consideration, the government has decided not to put up
   the price of ice-cream.

13 Don't you get annoyed .... people who push past you without saying
   "Excuse me"?

14 There's a man over there with binoculars. Do you think he's a birdwatcher, or
   is he spying .... us?

15 The public is taking a lot of interest .... the new courses being
   offered by the Open University.

16 Please, Father, may I go to the cinema with John tonight? .... all, I
   am twenty-three years old now.

17 Professor Jonah Newt is a specialist .... marine biology.

18 When I met my wife, it was love .... first sight. It was only later that
   I had second thoughts.

19 "Would you like a drink, officer?"
   "Not while I'm .... duty, sir."

20 Professor Newt is absorbed at the moment .... a study of the feeding
   habits of the whale.

Nouns following "on"

Complete the table on the right by filling in the blanks in the following sentences.

1 The soldiers had orders to shoot the deserter on ....

	I		T

2 "On no .... are you to accept lifts from strangers," said the mother to her young child.

	C				T

3 We'd all better arrive on .... tomorrow; otherwise we might miss the train.

	M	

4 I see Brian's put his house on .... Mind you, I don't think it'll be very easy to sell.

	A	

5 The suspect was released from prison on ....

B		

6 Your book hasn't come yet. But it's on ...., so it should arrive by Friday.

O			

7 "You're going to go on a long ....," said the fortune-teller.

	O	R		

8 I've put on a lot of weight lately. I think I'd better go on a .... again.

		T	

9 All her friends were busy, so she had to go to the party on her ....

	N	

10 Tonight is important. So remember, be on your best ....

B			V			R

11 Before buying anything, he sent for a sample on ....

	P	R		L	

12 I hate planning things; it's much more fun to do everything on ....

		P	L		

13 I never pay cash; I always buy on ....

	R			

14 Ms Temple isn't here this week. She's gone to Japan on ....

		S				S

15 Don't write to me between 1 and 16 June, as I shall be on .... then.

	O		D	

A well-known phrase or saying

List 1 consists of a number of common expressions (sayings and proverbs). Supply the missing preposition(s) and then match the expressions to the definitions given in List 2. (Some are used more than once.)

against	from	on	up
before	in	out of	with
between	into	over	without

LIST 1

1 A bird .... the hand is worth two .... the bush.

2 It's like banging your head .... a brick wall.

3 .... the devil and the deep blue sea.

4 Have a card .... your sleeve.

5 Have several irons .... the fire.

6 An iron hand .... a velvet glove.

7 It's no use crying .... spilt milk.

8 Keep the wolf .... the door.

9 Kill two birds .... one stone.

10 Make a mountain .... a molehill.

11 .... sight, ... mind.

12 .... the frying pan and .... the fire.

13 Put the cart .... the horse.

14 The grass is always greener .... the other side.

15 There's no smoke .... fire.

LIST 2

(a) Take advantage of one action to achieve something else as well.

(b) Surrounded by problems with no escape.

(c) There must be some truth in even the most unlikely rumour.

(d) Someone who appears to treat you gently but is hard and ruthless underneath.

(e) You can only be sure of what you have at the moment; you cannot be sure of something that you might get in the future.

(f) Exaggerate, make a big fuss over something that is not very serious.

(g) Do things in the wrong order.

(h) In negotiations, to have something in reserve that you have not yet revealed.

(i) Manage to earn just enough to live on.

(j) All your efforts are getting you nowhere.

(k) You no sooner get out of one difficulty than you find yourself in another just as bad.

(l) The tendency to believe that life would be better somewhere else.

(m) We easily forget people as soon as we are no longer with them.

(n) To have a number of different interests.

(o) You should not waste time regretting things that you cannot change.

45 Similar, but different

The following sentences each contain a prepositional phrase that could easily be confused with others, e.g., on time, in time, at a time, at times. In each case only one fits the sentence.

1 I advertised several times for someone to mow the lawn for me, but .... the end I had to do it myself.

   (a) in   **(b)** by   **(c)** at   **(d)** to

2 I'm sorry I can't see you immediately, but if you'd like to take a seat, I'll be with you .... moment.

   (a) for the   **(b)** at the   **(c)** in a   **(d)** for a

3 I didn't trust the post, so I delivered the parcel .... hand.

   (a) by   **(b)** to   **(c)** on   **(d)** out of

4 We've had such a busy day! At least ten people phoned. Oh, ... the way, there's a message here for you from your brother.

   (a) on   **(b)** in   **(c)** by   **(d)** over

5 If you want to be a professional spy, you must learn to be very secretive. .... all, you must learn to listen more and speak less.

   (a) In   **(b)** After   **(c)** At   **(d)** Above

6 His name is Sebastian, but we call him Seb .... short.

   (a) in   **(b)** for   **(c)** as   **(d)** by

7 I have some important information for you, but I don't want to give it .... the phone. Do you think we could meet somewhere?

   (a) by   **(b)** through   **(c)** on   **(d)** over

8 Is everything OK, sergeant?
   Don't worry, sir! Everything's .... control.

   (a) under   **(b)** in   **(c)** on   **(d)** by

9 Do you agree?
   .... point, but I don't think you are completely right.

   (a) To the   **(b)** For a   **(c)** Up to a   **(d)** On the

10 I never met Joe Louis, but he was a great boxer ....

   (a) by all accounts   **(b)** on account   **(c)** in the account
   (d) according to the accounts

11 I forgot to pack any food, so we'll get something to eat .... the way back.

(**a**) in   (**b**) all   (**c**) on   (**d**) by

12 The red light goes on outside the studio door to let people know that you are .... air.

(**a**) on the   (**b**) by   (**c**) in   (**d**) through the

13 The auditors have been through the accounts, and they report that everything is .... order.

(**a**) to   (**b**) on   (**c**) by   (**d**) in

14 Have you seen this morning's paper? There's a big picture of you .... the front!

(**a**) at   (**b**) on   (**c**) in   (**d**) by

15 "The other children all call me Big Head."
"Don't be so sensitive! You mustn't take everything .... heart! Now, run down to the greengrocer's and get me three kilos of potatoes in your cap."

(**a**) to   (**b**) by   (**c**) in your   (**d**) at

16 The general manager is away .... business this week.

(**a**) for   (**b**) on   (**c**) in   (**d**) about

17 I've taken this watch .... pieces, and now I can't put it together again.

(**a**) into   (**b**) to   (**c**) in   (**d**) out of

18 ".................. during the performance of this trick, ladies and gentlemen, do my hands actually leave my arms."

(**a**) On time   (**b**) In no time   (**c**) At no time   (**d**) At times

19 There is nothing illegal about my business dealings. Everything is strictly .... board.

(**a**) on   (**b**) above   (**c**) by the   (**d**) over

20 "Ah, sweet mystery of life .... I've found you!"

(**a**) at the last   (**b**) at least   (**c**) at last   (**d**) at the least

46 Word association 2

Each of the words and phrases on the left can be associated with one of the prepositional phrases on the right. Try to match them up correctly.

1	He broke the law!	**(a)**	in mourning
2	Don't tell anyone else!	**(b)**	on the agenda
3	Your valuables are safe!	**(c)**	at a moment's notice
4	Everyone wants it!	**(d)**	in the flesh
5	a fugitive	**(e)**	in gaol
6	His wife just died	**(f)**	out of step
7	a satellite	**(g)**	in the lead
8	a personal appearance	**(h)**	between you and me
9	Real Madrid lost again!	**(i)**	out of focus
10	He's winning!	**(j)**	in orbit
11	industrial dispute	**(k)**	under lock and key
12	a board meeting	**(l)**	on the air
13	a radio broadcast	**(m)**	in hiding
14	The picture's blurred!	**(n)**	off form
15	What a rush!	**(o)**	in demand
16	soldiers marching	**(p)**	on strike

Write your answers here:

1	2	3	4	5	6	7	8	9	10	11	12	13	14	15	16

Prepositions after verbs 3

Complete the sentences below with one of the following verbs plus a preposition. (Make any changes to verb tenses that may be necessary.)

abide	confine	decide	surround
account	count	grumble	specialise
accuse	cry	insist	taste
book	deal	refrain	translate

1 The teacher .... calling me Ghenghis, even though my real name is Attila.

2 Michael trained as a psychiatrist, and he now .... mental disorders of the very rich.

3 I was .... cheating in the examination, just because I had made a few notes on the back of my hand.

4 Scientists are unable to .... the sudden increase in sunspot activity, although some people believe that aerosols are to blame.

5 Footballers used to .... the referee's decision, but nowadays they are just as likely to punch him in the mouth.

6 The hotel's fire regulations have been .... eighteen languages, thereby ensuring that guests will burn to death while trying to find the version in their own language.

7 "My coffee .... garlic!"
   "You're lucky, mine has no taste at all."

8 The English .... the weather, but secretly they don't mind their climate, because they love complaining.

9 I was thinking of going to live in Scotland, but when I heard that I would have to wear a kilt, I .... it.

10 If there are any personnel problems in the factory, the boss always asks his deputy to .... them.

11 "Why am I .... idiots?"
   "We don't know, Father."

12 They used to say of Errol Flynn that you could .... him: he would always let you down.

13 It's no use .... spilt milk.

14 The kakapo is a rare flightless, nocturnal ground parrot. It is now .... South Island, New Zealand, which is another reason why most people have never seen one.

15 Passengers are kindly requested to .... smoking in the gangways and in the toilets.

16 As it was getting late, we decided to .... the nearest hotel.

48 What noun follows the preposition?

Complete the table on the right by filling in the blanks in the following sentences.

1. I don't mind a bit of fun, but putting salt in Grandma's coffee is beyond a ....

2. How long can you stay under .... before you have to come up for air?

3. John is in Saudi Arabia at ...., but he should be home next week.

4. Before we were married, you said that you would love me for ....

5. The idea looks good on ...., but will it really work?

6. The parcel that the postman threw on to my desk has FRAGILE, HANDLE WITH .... written on it.

7. The orchard is beautiful in spring, when all the fruit trees are in ....

8. I can see from your tie that you had a boiled egg for.................. .

9. When I went down on my .... and asked her to marry me, she said I was not tall enough.

10. I didn't get a rise: the boss said that it was out of the .... this year.

11. Practical training is often known as "on the ...." training.

12. This encyclopedia is out of ....: it says that the present ruler of France is a Corsican.

13. When the police told him he was under .... for bigamy, my grandfather was delighted.

14. The park is safe during the day, but you should not go there alone after ....

15. When you park, don't just put on the handbrake. Leave the car in .... as well.

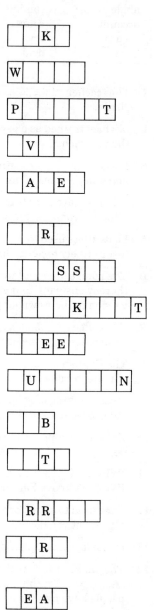

One word only   3

Read through the following and fill in the numbered blanks with one suitable word. Then decide if the story is true or false.

A Holiday Death

(1) .... a camping holiday (2) .... Spain, grandmother, who had been brought along (3) .... the (4) .... of the family, died suddenly (5) .... the night (6) .... natural causes. Not wanting to bury her (7) .... a foreign country, where they might never be able to visit her grave again, the family (8) .... to head (9) .... home and attempt to smuggle her (10) .... Spain and France and so (11) .... to England.

(12) .... this (13) .... mind, they rolled Grandmother's body (14) .... a carpet, tied it on to the roof rack (15) .... the car (16) .... with the camping equipment and started on their (17) ....

They drove all night and just (18) .... breakfast, they heaved a sigh of (19) .... as they crossed the border out of Spain and (20) .... France.

(21) .... this time, all the family were very tired and hungry. As a stop (22) .... breakfast sounded like a good idea, they parked the car (23) .... a side street (24) .... to a suitable café. Not wanting to leave the corpse (25) .... too long and also wishing to continue their journey as soon as possible, they ate a quick breakfast and (26) .... to the car. However, (27) .... their horror, their possessions had been stolen (28) .... the roof (29) .... the car, including the carpet and grandmother's corpse!

The strange thing is – the body never did turn (30) ....

50 Choose the preposition 6: by, for, of, on, to

*Complete the following sentences using **by, for, of, on** or **to**.*

1 I'm longing .... the summer holidays to arrive, aren't you?

2 John was about to take his wife out to dinner when it occurred ....
   him that he was not married.

3 You ought to be ashamed .... yourself!

4 *Hamlet* is a play .... William Shakespeare.

5 The Chairman called .... Mr Smith to second the motion.

6 You can change your job. You can move house. But marriage is ....
   life.

7 I'm sorry you have been expelled from the garden, Adam, but ....
   some extent it's your own fault.

8 What do you get if you divide 22 .... 7? A complicated number.

9 You can go to the disco tonight .... condition that you are home by 12
   o'clock.

10 Because of a lack .... interest, tomorrow has been cancelled.
    (Notice outside a theatre)

11 She was irritated .... the way her fiancé picked his nose, so she broke
    it off.

12 Take advantage .... this special offer! 50 per cent off list price while
    stocks last!

13 Because of the increase in the number of firms offering financial services,
    there's a bigger demand than ever .... qualified accountants.

14 Please give my regards .... your mother, Oedipus, when you see her
    again.

15 "I am Polish .... birth, but I have French nationality."
    "What do you do for a living?"
    "I'm a French polisher."

16 Congratulations .... your thirty-fifth birthday!

17 The railway police have finally arrested the man who has been responsible .... biting all the buttons off railway carriage seats.

18 With reference .... your advertisement in today's *Guardian*, I should like to apply for the post of Head Clerk in your Sales Department.

19 He went .... his own accord: nobody forced him to go.

20 Sarah is studying hard. She is intent .... getting a good degree.

Answers

TEST 1

1 opposite
2 on
3 under
4 above
5 to the left of
6 in front of
7 in
8 between
9 behind
10 inside
11 to the right of
12 below

TEST 2

1 for
2 by/at
3 at
4 for
5 at
6 for
7 for
8 in
9 by
10 for
11 in
12 at
13 for
14 at
15 in
16 at
17 for
18 by
19 in
20 at

TEST 3

1 during
2 in
3 on
4 from
5 for
6 after
7 in
8 in
9 On
10 on
11 by
12 behind
13 on
14 within
15 after
16 at
17 from
18 to
19 past
20 by
21 until
22 no preposition needed
23 in
24 since
25 for
26 no preposition needed
27 on
28 in

TEST 4

1 (h)
2 (d)
3 (p)
4 (l)
5 (i)
6 (m)
7 (e)
8 (c)
9 (f)
10 (j)
11 (a)
12 (n)
13 (g)
14 (b)
15 (k)
16 (o)

TEST 5

ACROSS
2 about
3 married
4 accustomed
8 sorry
9 afraid
11 good
12 successful
14 satisfied
18 suitable
19 with

DOWN
1 absent
5 covered
6 engrossed
7 typical
10 descended
11 grateful
13 fluent
15 tired
16 famous
17 guilty

TEST 6

1 (d) Why can't you hide <u>behind</u> a newspaper <u>at</u> breakfast like other husbands?
2 (h) What do you mean it's not that bad? I'm standing <u>on</u> my husband's shoulders!
3 (j) I think we'd better apologise <u>to</u> them <u>for</u> waking them up.
4 (f) I'm allergic <u>to</u> feathers, you see.
5 (c) You used to gaze <u>at</u> me like that!
6 (a) It's amazing <u>to</u> me how people always seem to get married in alphabetical order.
7 (e) What do you mean you can't sleep <u>with</u> the light on?
8 (i) This is the part I don't like – having to think <u>of</u> different names <u>for</u> them all.
9 (g) What a pity you haven't brought your little dog <u>with</u> you. We were so looking forward <u>to</u> seeing him again.
10 (b) Do I take it you object <u>to</u> my smoking a pipe?

TEST 7

1	(g)	9	(m)
2	(d)	10	(o)
3	(k)	11	(e)
4	(n)	12	(h)
5	(i)	13	(b)
6	(p)	14	(j)
7	(a)	15	(l)
8	(c)	16	(f)

TEST 8

1	in	25	between
2	to	26	owing
3	change	27	of
4	by	28	to
5	According	29	terms
6	from	30	on
7	at	31	between
8	on	32	in
9	in	33	making
10	in	34	with
11	from	35	in
12	coast	36	for
13	in	37	By
14	through	38	for
15	before	39	into
16	from	40	to
17	to	41	for
18	at	42	at
19	in	43	to
20	practice/reality/fact	44	In
21	start	45	after
22	To	46	on
23	with	47	from
24	of	48	of

TEST 9

1	speed	9	least
2	guess	10	night
3	distance	11	war
4	dawn	12	last
5	first	13	moment
6	home	14	risk
7	disadvantage	15	hand
8	discount		

TEST 10

1	off	15	to
2	along/down	16	before
3	towards	17	At
4	on	18	of
5	after	19	of
6	on	20	in
7	across/over/through	21	outside
8	along/down	22	round/around
9	through	23	for
10	at	24	to
11	along	25	of
12	to	26	under/inside
13	over/across	27	to
14	Behind		

TEST 11

1	at	11	against
2	about	12	about
3	from	13	from
4	at	14	at
5	about	15	against
6	against	16	about
7	from	17	against
8	about	18	from
9	at	19	at
10	from	20	against

TEST 12

1	capable of	9	involved in
2	bad at	10	aware of
3	inspired by	11	distracted by
4	adequate for	12	full of
5	addicted to	13	notorious for
6	jealous of	14	angry with
7	disqualified from	15	sympathetic to
8	expert at	16	eligible for

TEST 13

1	out of date	9	not for long
2	at times	10	in the end
3	before long	11	to this day
4	from now on	12	without delay
5	from time to time	13	at the moment
6	in season	14	for the time being
7	at length	15	In the meantime
8	in no time	16	in progress

TEST 14 (suggested answers)

1 Pisa is famous for its leaning tower.
2 This passport is valid for most countries.
3 They got married in secret.
4 Is Jennifer a relative of yours?
5 Would you care for a drink?
6 My cousin borrowed £5 from me.
7 A car collided with a bus this morning.

8   We were doubtful about her chances of passing the exam.
9   He had difficulty in opening the window.
10 Take no notice of what she says.
11 The painting has been valued at £25,000.
12 She is bored with her present job.
13 He died at the age of seventy-six.
14 She lived on the outskirts of the town.
15 He roared with laughter when he saw the clown.
16 Our customs are different from/to theirs.
17 I don't feel in the mood for going out tonight./I'm not in the mood for going out tonight.
18 She spent the evening by herself.

TEST 15

1   after ... After ... for
2   of
3   on
4   in ... at
5   in
6   At ... of
7   to ... by
8   of
9   in/into
10 with
11 for
12 at
13 for
14 on ... at ... with
15 of
16 from ... about ... in ... since

TEST 16

1	accident	9	dozen
2	appointment	10	force
3	means	11	surprise
4	boat	12	way
5	cheque	13	profession
6	law	14	marriage
7	name	15	nature
8	air		

TEST 17 (suggested answers)

1   I can see that my dog has really taken to you.
2   Would you like to elaborate on what you proposed at our last meeting?
3   Michael jumped at the chance to go to Australia.
4   Will my age count against me?
5   Where do you hail from? (i.e., the same as "come from")
6   Many people do not hold with women with small children going out to work.
7   The repairs we have had to do on the car have really eaten into our savings.
8   Tedious as it was, I had to plough through a large number of documents before I found what I was looking for.
9   She stumbled across the missing pearl necklace while she was looking for something else.
10 Any money I have to spare is put towards my holiday.
11 Everybody deserted John after he was arrested and put on trial for embezzlement, but his wife told him, "I will stick by you, John, whatever happens."
12 She decided to indulge in a bottle of expensive champagne to celebrate her promotion.
13 During the interview, the Prime Minister tried to gloss over the part of the story that he found embarrassing.
14 Everyone is raving about Lloyd Webber's latest musical.
15 I am happy to vouch for his integrity.
16 Little boys know how to get round their parents.

TEST 18

1 **in time** "on time" means "punctually": Sally always arrived on time for work.
2 **died of** You "die of" a disease; you "die from" injuries, a wound, etc.
3 **on the point of** "at the point of" means "close to": my grandfather is at the point of death.
4 **at the end** "in the end" means "eventually": he tried the exam several times and in the end he managed to pass.
5 **at heart** "by heart" means "from memory": prepositions should be learnt by heart.
6 **in time of** "at the time of" means "at a particular point in time": I was living in Sweden at the time of my mother's death.
7 **for fear of** When the army began shooting wildly, we ran in fear of our lives.
8 **friendly to** "friendly to" something, "friendly with" someone.
9 **divide it among** "divide between" when there are two people, "divide among" when there are more than two.
10 **in the possession of** "in possession of" means "having in one's possession": since we weren't in possession of all the details, we couldn't make a decision.
11 **clever at** "clever at" is followed by a verb, "clever with" is followed by a pronoun or noun: he is clever at making things; he is clever with his hands.
12 **care about** "care for" means "like" or "want": would you care for another cup of tea?
13 **by name** He's a true Johnson in everything but in name.
14 **angry at** "angry at" something, "angry with" someone.
15 **by sight** "on sight" means "as soon as you see someone": the police had orders to shoot on sight.
16 **in front of** there's a list of contents at the front of the book.
17 **in favour of** "in favour with" means "being liked by someone" or "having their approval": you can't expect to be in favour with your teacher if you never do your homework.
18 **in principle** "on principle" means "because of set or fixed beliefs": he refused to leave a tip on principle.
19 **in case of** "in the case of" means "regarding" or "with regard to": your getting the sack was unfair, but in the case of Paul it was quite justified.
20 **in view of** "with a view to" means "with the purpose or intention of": he bought the car with a view to repairing it and reselling it later.

TEST 19

1 **in his good books** Kevin was liked by the boss.
2 **on his last legs.** He's close to death.
3 **out of her hands** She is no longer in control.
4 **by word of mouth** It was passed on orally rather than through writing.
5 **in great demand** He is very popular; everyone wants to talk to him.
6 **in the clear** He is no longer suspected of the crime.
7 **up to her eyes in** She is extremely busy.
8 **at first hand** He learnt directly – from his own experience – what it was like to be hungry.
9 **at the eleventh hour** They arrived just in time; at the last possible moment.
10 **once in a blue moon** She goes rarely.
11 **on a shoestring** They lived on very little money.
12 **in a month of Sundays** He will never ever pass the exam.
13 **under the counter** They were available illegally.
14 **by a long chalk** There is still a long way to go before he wins.
15 **at her fingertips** She was very familiar with her subject.
16 **in dribs and drabs** They arrived in very small numbers, not all at once.
17 **at the double** Very quickly.
18 **get in a cold sweat** I get very frightened.
19 **on the level** It is the truth.
20 **from A to Z** I know the subject extremely well.

TEST 20

ACROSS		DOWN	
4	increase	1	cruelty
6	of	2	between
8	reputation	3	towards
11	difficulty	5	cheque
12	over	7	in
14	with	9	solution
16	against	10	from
17	recipe	13	engagement
19	quotation	15	advice
		18	for
		20	to

TEST 21

The two letters are as follows:

Letter 1

Dear Bob,
(1) Sorry I've taken such a long time in answering your letter, but the truth is that I've been really busy these past few weeks (2) with exams and everything, so I hope you understand.
  My main reason for writing, however, is to ask if you feel like spending a couple of weeks with us (3) in the summer? Mum and Dad have hired a caravan in Fairlight – a little village (4) near Hastings, and they thought you might like to join us for two weeks – from 2–15 August. It sleeps four, so there's plenty of room. And it's only five minutes (5) from the sea, so we could go swimming every day. It should be great fun, but it would be even better if you could be there too. So what do you say? Apart (6) from this, there's not much else to say really. Dad's got a new car – a Volvo – and Mum's just started back to work again.
  By the way, Dad asked me to find (7) out if your parents received the holiday brochures he sent, as he hasn't heard (8) from them yet.
  Well, Bob, that's all for now. I hope you're keeping well and that you'll be able to join us (9) in the summer.
  Give my regards to your parents and write soon.

Lots of love,

Paul

Letter 2

(a) Dear Paul,
Many thanks for your letter. It was nice to hear from you at last. (I was beginning to think you'd emigrated!)
  About the summer, yes (b) of course I'd love to join you and your parents in Fairlight. It sounds really fun. I visited Hastings once and it was a really nice place – lots (c) of things to do and so on – especially in the summer. (Lots of pretty foreign students too!) So thank your parents for me and tell them I'm really looking forward to it.
  I asked Mum and Dad (d) about the holiday brochures, and they say they haven't received them yet. (Well, you know what the post is like!) But they'll write as soon as they get them, and they asked me to tell you to thank your dad (e) for all the trouble he's gone to.
  By the way, Paul, Dad's very jealous (f) of the new Volvo. He's always liked foreign cars – especially Volvos – and keeps hinting (g) to Mum about getting a new car. But she's not interested, really, so I don't think he'll persuade her.
  Well, Paul, I'll stop now because I'm off to a disco (h) with Sally. You remember Sally, don't you? She was the girl I met at Jenny's birthday party. We've been together now (i) for almost three months. (Not bad for me!) What about you? Are you still going out with Pauline or have you got someone new now?
  Anyway, do write some time and remember to give my love (j) to your mum and dad.

Lots of love,

Bob

P.S.
Don't forget you're coming here (k) for my birthday party on the nineteenth. (Bring Pauline, if you like!)

TEST 22

1	work	9	compensation
2	a cost	10	behalf
3	peace	11	good terms
4	means	12	pity
5	the benefit	13	the accompaniment
6	aid	14	the influence
7	agreement	15	reference
8	answer	16	the compliments

TEST 23

1	in	11	over
2	over	12	into
3	on	13	on
4	into	14	in
5	over	15	into/onto
6	in	16	over
7	on	17	in
8	into	18	on
9	over	19	into
10	in	20	on

TEST 24

1	summer	9	code
2	condition	10	confidence
3	mood	11	danger
4	hurry	12	debt
5	advance	13	bed
6	emergency	14	conclusion
7	taste	15	moderation
8	case		

TEST 25 (suggested answers)

1 I used to have a car that is similar to yours.
2 He is incapable of telling a lie.
3 Mary had a craving for jelly when she was pregnant.
4 My boss takes great pleasure in humiliating people
or
My boss gets a lot of pleasure out of/from humiliating people.
5 I am not in the habit of speaking to strange men.
6 Sarah made a very good impression on the interview panel.
7 Irish history is the key to understanding/an understanding of Yeats's poetry.
8 John is crazy about sports cars.
9 I have been deserted by all my friends.
10 I have confidence in my best friend.
11 Henry had a talent for making people laugh.
12 The moon is made of green cheese, according to my father.
13 Long noses are (a) characteristic of the people of Dolichorrinia.
14 I can recite the whole of Wordsworth's *Prelude* from memory.
15 The items you want are out of stock/no longer/not in stock.
16 I am very grateful to you for your help/for helping me.
17 I work best (when I am/when you put me) under pressure.
18 Kate is popular with all the teachers.

TEST 26

1	hear about	7	suffered from	12	belongs to
2	vote against	8	experiment on/with	13	rhymes with
3	arrived at	9	losing at	14	knocking at
4	distinguish between	10	complained to	15	apologised to
5	pray for	11	corresponds to	16	leave/are leaving for
6	died from				

TEST 27

1 away for
2 down with
3 away with
4 over to
5 down to
6 out for
7 behind with
8 around to
9 up to
10 in for
11 around for
12 back on
13 up with
14 on at
15 up on
16 in with

TEST 28

1 for/on
2 in
3 for
4 on
5 of
6 no preposition needed
7 for/in
8 at
9 in
10 from
11 of
12 about
13 about
14 in
15 from
16 to
17 in
18 of
19 with
20 at/in
21 into
22 with
23 on
24 of
25 no preposition needed
26 into/in
27 in
28 to/up to
29 to
30 of/in
31 to/at
32 on
33 from
34 about/of
35 at (meaning he was a student at the university. "In" would mean that he just happened to be in the town.)
36 about
37 in
38 to
39 no preposition
40 about
41 for
42 no preposition
43 to
44 on
45 to
46 into
47 for
48 from
49 no preposition
50 into
51 from
52 of
53 in
54 of
55 no preposition
56 of/at
57 into
58 in
59 unlike
60 for
61 For
62 of
63 under(neath)/beneath
64 with (or no preposition)
65 at/by
66 in
67 of
68 around/above
69 at
70 to
71 off
72 with

TEST 29

1 choice between
2 opposite of
3 campaign against
4 objection to
5 trouble with
6 excuse for
7 knowledge of
8 freedom from
9 control over
10 cruelty to
11 strain on
12 fall in
13 genius at
14 basis for
15 grudge against
16 news to

TEST 30

ACROSS

2	prefers
6	travelled
9	shouting
10	among
11	on
12	into
13	in
14	between
16	against
17	from
20	multiply
21	from
22	with

DOWN

1	shelter
3	for
4	exchange
5	join
7	about
8	escape
12	invited
15	worry
18	blame
19	mixing
21	flow
23	to

TEST 31

AT
glance
hint
marvel
point
wink

ON
bet
concentrate
depend
rely
tread

FROM
abstain
benefit
depart
expel
flee

TO
appeal
dedicate
subscribe
object
respond

IN
believe
decrease
delight
indulge
invest

WITH
coincide
collaborate
cope
quarrel
sympathise

OF
approve
consist
dispose
dream
take advantage

TEST 32

1	With	**11**	in
2	to	**12**	with
3	out of	**13**	under
4	under	**14**	out of
5	in	**15**	under
6	with	**16**	to
7	out of	**17**	in
8	in	**18**	to
9	under	**19**	out of
10	to	**20**	with

TEST 33

1	detail	9	disguise
2	hospital	10	focus
3	existence	11	love
4	opinion	12	pain
5	difficulty	13	doubt
6	fact	14	fashion
7	future	15	general
8	comfort		

TEST 34

The two letters are as follows:

Letter 1

(1) Dear Sir,
I wish to make a complaint about a recent holiday to Copenhagen. According to the brochure I received (2) from Sunthoms Holidays, the holiday was to include a two-day boat trip to Oslo (3) in Norway. However, what your brochure failed to mention was the fact that the excursion was to be paid (4) for separately! Unfortunately, our travel representative forgot to mention this fact until we were well at sea! By (5) that time it was too late to change one's mind. And had I realised how much it was going to cost, I would certainly not have gone on it – especially since the sea was so choppy that my wife and I spent most (6) of the trip being seasick!

I would be grateful if you could make sure in (7) future that all "extra" costs are clearly shown in your brochure.

Apart (8) from the above, the rest of our holiday in Copenhagen was wonderful, and both my wife and I fell in love (9) with the Tivoli Gardens. What an experience! What an atmosphere! And to think that it's in the centre (10) of the city. Whatever happens, we shall certainly try to return to Copenhagen at (11) some future date. (I can't say the same about Oslo!)

Yours faithfully,

Bernard Wilson

Letter 2

(a) Dear Sir,
I have just returned from a holiday in Spain and all I can say is that it was a nightmare from (b) start to finish! When I chose Sunthoms Holidays I was under the impression that I was dealing (c) with a company you could rely on. How wrong can you be!

The trouble started even before (d) we had left the country. To begin with, the plane was overbooked. This meant that myself and ten other passengers were forced to go on another plane – one hour later! Unfortunately, our luggage was still (e) on the first plane, so that there was a further delay in (f) sorting out the mess when we finally arrived at the airport in Spain.

The "luxury" hotel as advertised in your holiday brochure was still under (e) construction, which meant that there was the constant sound of cement mixers and so on – hardly the peaceful and relaxing holiday I had been looking forward to.

My room was much smaller than I had expected and throughout (h) my stay I never once managed to get the shower to work properly – the water was either too cold or too hot.

Another thing, in your brochure you state that the hotel is only a few minutes from (i) the sea. Twenty-five to be exact! And what a beach. It was so polluted that it was positively dangerous (j) to one's health.

Finally, on the return journey I found myself sitting (k) amongst a group of smokers despite the fact that I had specifically asked for a non-smoking seat. If I get lung cancer in (l) the future then all I can say is that Sunthoms Holidays are to blame! This is the worst holiday I have ever had in my life, and I demand to get my money back. If not, I shall put the matter in the hands of my solicitor.

I look forward (m) to hearing from you soon.

Yours faithfully,

Ms Pauline Wood

TEST 35

1	in ... at ... into
2	for ... of
3	into ... of ... in
4	in ... of
5	in ... with
6	in
7	on
8	from

9	for
10	on ... into ... to
11	(in)to ... of ... through
12	into
13	on
14	for ... to
15	over
16	for ... for

TEST 36

1	pressed on
2	jump to
3	pay for
4	calls on
5	reason with
6	fuss over
7	begs for
8	concealing from

9	perish by
10	apply for
11	grow on
12	flock to
13	sharing in
14	prying into
15	dates from

TEST 37

1	exchange
2	common
3	addition
4	favour
5	odds
6	the expense

7	regard
8	the exception
9	the sake
10	respect
11	account
12	virtue

TEST 38

1 (c) So much for "enriched with vitamins and energy-giving minerals"!
2 (e) Are you related to the Smiths in rooms 102, 110, 120, 130 and 141 by any chance?
3 (i) Sorry – we don't have a menu. Just point at/to something on my apron.
4 (a) Arthur's always been very sensitive about his bald spot.
5 (g) Actually, this is number 13. Number 14 is just round the corner.
6 (j) I've decided against becoming a doctor – you have to wash your hands too often.
7 (f) Living in the past again, Harold?
8 (b) I'm not at my best first thing in the morning.
9 (h) Is the banging on the wall keeping you awake, darling?
10 (d) And, above all, madam, my party believes in total honesty in politics.

TEST 39

1	clever with
2	sensitive to
3	envious of
4	quick at
5	accompanied by
6	deep in
7	famous for
8	peculiar to

9	allergic to
10	surprised at
11	ahead of
12	faced with
13	fortunate in
14	descended from
15	exempt from
16	worthy of

TEST 40

2, 7, 12, 14, 17, 4, 1, 9, 18, 5, 11, 16, 13, 10, 15, 6, 8, 3

TEST 41 (suggested answers)

1 Anyone can apply for a job with us irrespective of race, creed or colour.
2 The film *Citizen Kane* has had a big impact on many film-makers.
3 My house is very handy for the station.
4 Our prices are subject to increase without warning.
5 Smoking in restaurant kitchens is contrary to Section Six of the Health and Safety Act.
6 She shot the intruder in self-defence.
7 A number of books are missing from the library.
8 I was disgusted at/by the way you spoke to your sister.
9 There are no exceptions to this rule.
10 Are you acquainted with the works of the poet William McGonagall?
11 There is a big/increased demand for automatic cars these days.
12 Lloyds Bank has no connection with Lloyds the Butcher's.
13 We are short of money to live on.
14 The provisions of the Wildlife Protection Act do not apply to pest species.
15 John is an expert on organic farming.
16 We ran into a barn to shelter/take shelter from the rain.
17 I am on very good terms with my bank manager.
18 Your pearl earrings are identical to mine.

TEST 42

1	on	11	on
2	off	12	After
3	at	13	at
4	in	14	on
5	after	15	in
6	on	16	After
7	at	17	in
8	after	18	at
9	at	19	on
10	in	20	in

TEST 43

1	sight	9	own
2	account	10	behaviour
3	time	11	approval
4	sale	12	impulse
5	bail	13	credit
6	order	14	business
7	journey	15	holiday
8	diet		

TEST 44

1	(e)	in	9	(a)	with	
2	(j)	against	10	(f)	out of	
3	(b)	Between	11	(m)	Out of ... out of	
4	(h)	up	12	(k)	Out of ... into	
5	(n)	in	13	(g)	before	
6	(d)	in	14	(l)	on	
7	(o)	over	15	(c)	without	
8	(i)	from				

TEST 45

1	(a)	11	(c)
2	(c)	12	(a)
3	(a)	13	(d)
4	(c)	14	(b)
5	(d)	15	(a)
6	(b)	16	(b)
7	(d)	17	(b)
8	(a)	18	(c)
9	(c)	19	(b)
10	(a)	20	(c)

TEST 46

1	(e)	9	(n)
2	(h)	10	(g)
3	(k)	11	(p)
4	(o)	12	(b)
5	(m)	13	(l)
6	(a)	14	(i)
7	(j)	15	(c)
8	(d)	16	(f)

TEST 47

1	insists on	9	decided against
2	specialises in	10	deal with
3	accused of	11	surrounded by
4	account for	12	count on
5	abide by	13	crying over
6	translated into	14	confined to
7	tastes of	15	refrain from
8	grumble about	16	book into

TEST 48

1	joke	9	knees
2	water	10	question
3	present	11	job
4	ever	12	date
5	paper	13	arrest
6	care	14	dark
7	blossom	15	gear
8	breakfast		

TEST 49

1	During	16	along/together
2	in	17	journey
3	with	18	before
4	rest/remainder	19	relief/joy/happiness
5	during/in	20	into
6	of	21	By
7	in	22	for
8	decided/determined	23	in
9	for/back	24	next
10	through	25	for
11	back	26	returned
12	With	27	to
13	in	28	from
14	in	29	of
15	of	30	up

The story is false. It is taken from a book called *The Book of Nasty Legends* by Paul Smith (Routledge). The book is full of so-called "true" stories.

TEST 50

1	for	11	by
2	to	12	of
3	of	13	for
4	by	14	to
5	on	15	by
6	for	16	on
7	to	17	for
8	by	18	to
9	on	19	of
10	of	20	on